MUNICH '72 AND BEYOND

MUNICH '72 AND BEYOND

A SAGA OF REDEMPTION. A MONUMENT OF REMEMBRANCE.
BASED ON THE AWARD-WINNING FILM

DAVID ULICH, STEPHEN UNGERLEIDER, AND **MICHAEL CASCIO**

DUNHAM
books

MUNICH '72 AND BEYOND

www.dunhamgroupinc.com

Hardcover ISBN: 978-0-9973973-6-9
Paperback ISBN: 978-0-9973973-5-2
eBook ISBN: 978-0-9973973-7-6

Library of Congress Control Number: 2018941130

Printed in the United States of America

CONTENTS

INTRODUCTION

"Let us not forget what happened here in 1972 so that it will never happen again."

–Ankie Spitzer, widow of Israeli fencing coach Andre Spitzer

David Ulich and Steven Ungerleider, authors of Munich '72 and Beyond

IN SEPTEMBER OF 1972, we joined sports enthusiasts around the world who tuned into the international broadcast of the Summer Olympics in Munich, West Germany. We witnessed glorious moments by star Olympians, like American swimmer Mark Spitz who won seven gold medals and broke seven world records. And Olga Korbut, the tiny Soviet gymnast called the "Sparrow of Minsk," who dazzled the crowd with her breathtaking acrobatics and transformed her sport in the process.

But ten days into competition, we were captivated by an altogether horrific spectacle as we witnessed the first act of modern terrorism unfold on live television. On September 5, 1972, eight Palestinian terrorists infiltrated the Olympic Village and took eleven Israeli athletes hostage, killing two of them almost immediately. After twenty-one excruciating hours, the other nine hostages and a German police officer also lost their lives. The devastated survivors of the Israeli Olympic delegation went home, and the Games went on.

Other athletes from several different countries also left in fear of potential terrorist activity. America's most prominent

American swimmer Mark Spitz won a record seven gold medals in Munich.
(Photo by Rolls Press/Popperfoto/Getty Images.)

athlete, Mark Spitz, who is Jewish, was flanked with armed guards until US officials had him flown home under Secret Service protection.

All of us were glued to our television sets as this drama played out. We can still see the iconic image of the terrorist in the gray ski mask, peering over the edge of the balcony. We can still hear Jim McKay's calm voice announcing the worst: "They're all gone." We remain, to this day, haunted by the kidnapping and murder of those eleven Israeli athletes.

The joyous exhibition of Munich's "Happy Games" became a bloody political showcase, and what was later known as the Munich massacre quickly became a pivot point for international politics, counterterrorism, and security protocols at every subsequent Olympic games—a sporting event meant to transcend all politics.

MUNICH'S ONGOING RELEVANCE

Much of the worldwide audience who watched the Munich Olympics likely had no idea who the Palestinians were—which was exactly why these assassins commandeered a global sports festival to ensure they and their cause were made known.

The group that attacked the Israeli athletes in Munich belonged to an extreme faction of the Palestinian Liberation Organization (PLO) called Black September, which took its name from a bloody war with the Jordan military just two years prior to the Munich Olympics. On September 6, 1970, Palestinian terrorists attempted to simultaneously hijack four commercial airliners flying from Europe to New York City. One hijacking was thwarted, but the three other jets were successfully redirected to Jordan, where passengers were held hostage and the empty planes blown up. The incident led to a battle between the PLO and Jordanian forces in Amman a week later, which killed thousands of Palestinians and expelled the PLO from the country.

Domestic and international airliner hijackings were increasingly common in that era, and on September 11, 1970, President Richard Nixon vowed measures

The terrorist in a gray ski mask became an iconic image of the attack.
(Russell McPhedran/The Sydney Morning Herald/Fairfax Media via Getty Images)

to finally combat "air piracy," which would eventually result in air marshals on planes and metal screeners in airports—the earliest paving of the road that leads to airport security as we know it today. Arab terrorism, however, was still considered to be primarily a regional threat in the Middle East—until Munich.

Black September's attack on the Olympic athletes was entirely unprecedented. According to national security expert Tim Naftali, the terms counterterrorism and international terrorism formally entered the Washington political lexicon after the events in Munich, as the US government established its first interagency working groups and cabinet-level committees to address the emergent threat.[1]

A *Time* magazine article published shortly after the Israeli athletes were murdered presciently stated, "Perhaps the ultimate significance of last week's horror in Munich is that the historic, bloody conflict between the Israelis and Arabs has now been exported from the Middle East to the rest of the world, first to Western Europe, and *maybe eventually even to the US* [emphasis ours]."[2]

Munich came to be seen as the harbinger of a new danger to US security.[3] But it wouldn't be treated as a strategic threat until another extremist group successfully hijacked four airplanes on September 11, 2001, an eerie echo of Black September's nascence.

A FIGHT FOR JUSTICE, A PLEA FOR REMEMBRANCE

While Black September's operations as a terrorist faction ceased only a couple of years after the attack in Munich, the pain the group inflicted has endured ever since.

For decades after the atrocities, the families of the slain Israelis, including widows Ankie Spitzer and Ilana Romano, tirelessly petitioned German officials for answers to what went down that dark day, but Germany refused to release reports or investigative documentation by denying that such files even existed. Only after twenty years of pleading and litigation against the German government did Ankie finally receive a bulging folder of files, smuggled out by an anonymous but empathetic source, that revealed details so horrific she and the other widows kept them secret for twenty more years—until their disclosure in their interviews with us for the *Munich '72 and Beyond* documentary.

At every ensuing Olympic Games, the victims' surviving family members relentlessly entreated the International Olympic Committee (IOC) for recognition of this devastating loss—a memorial service, a moment of silence—but they were instead given every conceivable excuse: it's in the past, it's politically inconvenient, it's just too somber. Justice and remembrance for their loved ones remained painfully elusive.

David Ulich, Steven Ungerleider, and Melanie Raffle of the Foundation for Global Sports Development have been an integral part of the international Olympic community for four decades. We have attended fourteen Olympiads where we often encountered athletes, coaches, administrators, and members of the IOC who were in Munich when the massacre happened and wanted to share their experiences. We also met the surviving family members at these Olympic events and at small, impromptu memorial services that were held to honor the memory of their lost loved ones. Through the years, we have guarded their stories close to our hearts, and we realized that the Olympic community needed to come to terms with this horrific trauma before any healing could take place.

More than four decades of advocacy and four IOC presidents later, the surviving family members of the Israelis killed in Munich, who were by then three generations deep, finally found their champion in Dr. Thomas Bach, who became the IOC president in 2013. A gold-medalist Olympian and longtime member of the Olympic movement, Dr. Bach knew the slain Israelis and their

The Foundation for Global Sports Development

families, and it troubled him for years that there was no closure to their tragedy. After taking office, one of his first initiatives was to pledge the IOC's full support to the Munich Massacre Memorial project, which had been established by the Bavarian State Ministry of Education, Science and Culture in 2012, and to initiate official commemoration of the eleven Olympians during the 2016 Rio Olympics.

Given our extensive involvement in the Olympic community, Dr. Bach asked us to be a liaison between the various parties involved in the Munich Massacre Memorial project—foreign ministries, the IOC, and the German and Israeli delegations. The IOC and the Foundation for Global Sports Development also pledged substantial financial support toward the memorial's construction costs.

We all shared a common vision: to create a place for remembrance, mourning, and healing. The memorial honors the heroism of the Israeli athletes and acknowledges the profound loss felt by their teammates and families. We hope this space, which sits just three hundred yards from where the Israeli athletes were held hostage, will also facilitate greater understanding between people from various nationalities, cultures, and religious faiths who can find a common denominator in the spirit of sportsmanship and the Olympic ideals.

A FILM IDEA WAS BORN

After several trips back and forth to Munich to participate in the planning meetings and architectural competitions for the memorial, an idea began to emerge. While we were on a return flight to the US, we mulled over the abiding significance of the Munich memorial and decided there was more to this project. There was a film in it as well. We needed to tell the story of how this memorial came to be.

The driving force behind the documentary was not to just re-create the events

*The **Munich '72 and Beyond** documentary has been viewed by millions of people around the world. (Design by Brand Navigation)*

in Munich, but to tie them to the memorial's creation and demonstrate why the memorial is such a crucial tribute. To that end, we partnered with award-winning filmmaker Stephen Crisman and executive producer Michael Cascio to tell the story of the massacre, the decades of controversy surrounding the survivors' requests for remembrance, and the makings of the memorial itself.

The result of our collaboration was *Munich '72 and Beyond*, which revisits that tragic day in September through the chilling words of eyewitnesses, journalists, authorities, and the victims' loved ones. The film exposes for the first time previously suppressed information about how the captors treated their hostages, the egregious failures of the German police force during the rescue attempt, and the victims' families' four-decade struggle for justice and recognition. We also felt it important to include the Palestinian perspective on the mindset of the terrorist faction. Even today, understanding one's enemies—their motives and goals—is crucial to preventing the vio-

lence they may be willing to inflict to achieve those ends.

The film won best documentary at the Los Angeles International Short Film Festival, which made the documentary eligible for an Academy Award. The film was first screened at the Sarasota Film Festival and since then has been selected for eighteen other festivals, including the St. Louis International Film Festival, Hawaii Shorts Fest, and the Toronto International Short Film Fest. The film won best documentary at the 2017 Euro Shorts International Film Festival.

David Ulich and Steven Ungerleider were nominated for an Emmy in the category of Outstanding Research for the *Munich '72 and Beyond* film at the 38th Annual News and Documentary Emmy Awards held in New York City on October 5, 2017.

We screened the documentary to thousands of viewers in thirty-eight Holocaust centers and museums in cities all over the US and around the world, including Paris, Prague, Munich, Jerusalem, and Tel Aviv. On television, 3.2 million people saw *Munich '72 and Beyond* via PBS stations in the US, and an unquantifiable number around the world by PBS international syndication. The film remains in distribution and will reach many more viewers in the coming years.

It is our hope that *Munich '72 and Beyond* will continue to shock, educate, and inspire audiences at museums, libraries, and cultural institutions for years to come.

To learn more about the memorial and the documentary, visit munichmemorial.org.

ABOUT THIS BOOK

Just when we thought we knew the whole story of the Munich massacre, a new chapter would unfold, a new character would emerge, a new document would be uncovered. Throughout the production process, we were given access to previously unavailable information about the shootout, and details from hidden files emerged from lawsuits

and special investigations that revealed shocking evidence of professional misconduct and negligence in trying to protect the athletes.

While interviewing the family members of the slain Israelis—their widows, siblings, sons, and daughters—we were moved to tears by their stories of strength, perseverance, rejection, and pain as they sought recognition for their lost loved ones. Though we couldn't fit every story into the film, we hope to illustrate in these pages a fuller scope of the people whose lives were shattered following this horrendous massacre.

In Part One, we reveal the gruesome facts of what happened that terrible day in September, from West Germany's hopes for "Happy Games" to the darkness and chaos of the final showdown at Fürstenfeldbruck airfield.

In Part Two, we lay out the accusations against the German authorities for the failure of the police maneuver. We also describe the survivors' four-decade-long fight for justice and their agony from being turned down each time they asked the IOC to remember their loved ones at the Olympics.

In Part Three, we celebrate the rise of Dr. Thomas Bach as a positive change agent in the IOC. We also showcase how the memorial's design supports private reflection and public remembrance, and how renowned architects put heart and soul into crafting a place for healing.

We believe deeply that the Olympic movement represents the highest ideals of peace and athleticism, and the terrorist attack on the Israeli athletes in Munich grossly betrayed those standards. By addressing it head on, let us as a global community make sure nothing like this ever happens again.

There is no room for terrorism at the Olympic Games.

There is no room for terrorism in the world.

Thanks to Dr. Bach, the victims of the Munich massacre and their loved ones were finally given the voice they long deserved. We intend to amplify that voice through the *Munich '72 and Beyond* film and this companion volume. Ultimately, the Munich Massacre Memorial is a very human story—but above all, it's *their* story—the innocent athletes who were slaughtered and their loved ones who navigated four decades of politics to secure an overdue moment of redemption for what seemed like a hopelessly irredeemable tragedy.

And as a footnote to history: during the Opening Ceremonies of the 2018 PyeongChang Winter Games in South Korea, while the Israeli delegation entered the arena, NBC sportscasters announced that the Munich Massacre Memorial had opened in Bavaria to honor those who were murdered on Olympic soil.

May their hearts at last find rest, may none of us ever forget them, and may their memories be for a blessing.

PART 1

THE MUNICH MASSACRE

CHAPTER 1

THE HAPPY GAMES

"We saw the tanks in the village; we saw the helicopters overhead. We knew this was a major act of terrorism, and we were in the middle of it."

—Barry Maister, former field hockey Olympian and New Zealand IOC member

ON A SUNNY SATURDAY IN 1972, the Olympic delegation from Israel, clad in blue blazers, red ties, and white hats, marched behind their flag into a grand stadium to join athletes from 120 other nations in the Opening Ceremony of the Summer Olympics in Munich, West Germany. Though the team had participated in five previous Olympics since becoming a nation in 1948, these Games—just twenty-seven years after World War II—were especially profound.

"Israel was young, almost a baby country. And for the generation who grew up then, it was the first steps of being a normal nation," said Noam Schiller, former special operative in the Israel Defense Forces and founder of Max Security Solutions, an intelligence and security services company headquartered in Tel Aviv. "These were Holocaust survivors, or the kids of Holocaust survivors. For them, it was a big thing as Jewish athletes coming with their heads up to join the Olympic games within Germany. It was a big thing here in the media and in people's hearts."

Noam Schiller, former Israeli special ops and founder of Max Security Solutions

The Israeli Olympic delegation marches in the 1972 Munich Opening Ceremony.
(Photo by Keystone-France/Gamm-Keystone via Getty Images.)

Diplomatic relations between Germany and Israel had been established for just seven years. Both Israelis and West Germans were, in this moment of pageantry, looking with hope and optimism toward the future, and not to the past. After ten days of competition, however, the vibrant, cheerful sports festival became entirely overshadowed by an atrocity none of them could have fathomed.

FROM THE NAZI OLYMPICS TO THE HAPPY GAMES

The 1972 Summer Olympics in Munich were the first Games to be held in Germany since 1936, when Berlin hosted the Summer Games and Adolf Hitler used the global platform to promote the racist and anti-Semitic ideologies of the Third Reich. Several nations proposed a boycott of the 1936 Summer Games, including France, Sweden, Great Britain, the former Czechoslovakia, and the Netherlands, with the strongest opposition coming from the United States. These efforts were short-lived, however, as leaders such as Avery Brundage insisted that politics had no place in sports.[4]

The 1936 Berlin Games were best remembered as Hitler's attempt to promote his theories of Aryan racial superiority.
(Photo by ullstein bild/ullstein bild via Getty Images)

German officials allowed only one Jewish athlete to represent Germany in Berlin—silver-medalist fencer Helene Mayer, whose father was Jewish.[5] In addition to Mayer, eight other athletes who were Jewish or had Jewish heritage won medals in the Nazi Olympics.[6] Jesse Owens, an African-American, won four

Adolf Hitler presides over the 1936 Berlin Summer Games. *(Photo by ullstein bild/ullstein bild via Getty Images)*

gold medals, a fact said to annoy Hitler, who had hoped the Games would showcase Nazi views on racial supremacy.

Only a few years after the 1936 Berlin Olympics, Hitler instigated a devastating world war and the murder of six million Jews.

Thirty-six years after the Nazi Olympics, West Germany was anxious to cleanse the image of its bloody, totalitarian past and present itself as a modern, free, democratic country.

For the authors, the Munich Games were a vivid memory of our youth.

"I was twelve years old in 1972, and my family bought our first color television just to watch the Munich Games," said David Ulich, one of the producers for

Munich '72 and Beyond. "My parents were German, so we found it exciting that the Games were being held in Munich. My grandparents, Elsa Brändström, Robert Ulich, and Else Ulich Beil were once members of the German Social Democratic party and escaped to the US when Hitler rose to power."

"My grandparents were both German Jews," added Dr. Steven Ungerleider, also a producer for the film. "Many of my relatives had to escape the death camps. My great-great-grandfather, Dr. Rudolf Ungerleider, was chief rabbi of Berlin at the turn of the century, and he's now buried in a small cemetery in the center of the city."

This was now a different Munich. To place the 1972 Summer Games in historical context, we recruited Jeremy Schaap, sportswriter and author of *Triumph: The Untold Story of Jesse Owens and Hitler's Olympics*, for the *Munich '72 and Beyond* documentary.

"The Olympics returning to Germany for the first time since before World War II—

Jeremy Schaap

before the Holocaust—was significant," explained Schaap. "The organizers of the 1972 Summer Games embraced the Munich event as an opportunity to supersede the imagery of Hitler's pomp and circumstance in Berlin. It was an opportunity to present a different face of Germany—not a martial Germany, but a peaceful Germany, a Germany interested in maintaining a place among the nations of the world, rather than superior to other nations of the world."

The Munich Olympics carried the official motto *Glückliche Spiele*—the Happy Games. The atmosphere was open and carefree, and in contrast to the blazes of red and black that cloaked the stands during the Nazi Olympics, Munich took a softer, lighter approach, with pale blue in its logo and uniforms. Bavarian officials and Olympic organizers were eager to please their international

Top: Olympiapark, the campus of the 1972 Munich Summer Olympics. (Christof Stache/AFP/Getty Images)

Above: Cheerleaders at the opening ceremony of the XX Olympiad, known as the Happy Games, Munich, 1972. (Mario De Biasi; Sergio Del Grande; Giorgio Lotti/Mondadori Portfolio via Getty Images)

guests and to promote peace and friendship among participants.

Peter Bonventre

"The Germans had really gone out of their way to make these Games perfect," said Peter Bonventre, a journalist who covered the Munich Olympics for *Newsweek* magazine. "The Games were exciting. The facilities were terrific. They had so many people helping you, guiding you, advising you. Everything was spic-and-span. Everything worked on time. It was just marvelous."

The Olympic Village teemed with athletes, coaches, and officials from all over the world. People of differing nationalities and ethnic groups struck up conversations, shared meals, played together, and watched movies and television programs together. The convivial community captured one of the ideals of the Olympic movement, in which politics and strife were suspended beyond its walls.

Ankie Spitzer

One afternoon, Andre Spitzer, the fencing coach for the Israeli team, strolled through the Olympic Village with his wife, Ankie. The couple had been married for just over a year and had a baby daughter, Anouk, who was born a few weeks prior to the Games. Ankie remembers an exchange between her husband and another coach that epitomized Andre's belief that the Olympic Games were a sanctuary apart from politics—a safe haven from war.

"We were in the Olympic Village, and my husband said, 'Hey, that's the Lebanese fencing team. I'm going to talk to them,'" Ankie told us during interviews for the documentary. "I said to him, 'Are you out of your mind? Israel is in a state of war with Lebanon.' And he said,

Ankie and Andre Spitzer on their wedding day. *(Photo courtesy of Ankie Spitzer)*

Andre Spitzer holds his newborn daughter, Anouk. *(Photo courtesy of Ankie Spitzer)*

'Ankie, this is the Olympics. Here, it is possible.' And I stayed a little behind, and he went toward them. They shook hands, and they were talking about the results and how wonderful it was there.

And he came to me and said, 'You see, there are no borders; there is no war. This is what the Olympics are all about.'" The West Germans' desire to foster such openness resulted in low-key security at the Olympic site in Munich, especially at the Olympic Village. Credentials were not checked closely at the gates. There were two thousand security officers around the Olympic venues, all dressed in pale blue uniforms but armed with nothing more than walkie-talkies.[7] As a result, the athletes' compound was left vulnerable, and in the end, West Germany's hopes for happy and carefree Games were shattered.

"They were not going to have anybody goose-stepping down the street as they did back in Berlin thirty-six years earlier," said Schaap. "This won't look like a fascist fantasy come to life, but a modern, democratic, forward-looking Germany. In so doing, they made the Games vulnerable. There wasn't enough security. There weren't enough guns. They ended up being directly responsible for what came next because of their lax security approach."

AN UNEXPECTED INFILTRATION

Before daybreak on Tuesday, September 5, eight Palestinians stood outside the Olympic Village near Gate A25, looking to get in. They were dressed in tracksuits in order to pass as athletes, but inside their large, black gym bags was an arsenal of handguns, grenades, and Russian-made Kalashnikov submachine guns. Around the time they arrived at the gate, which was locked but unguarded, the Palestinians encountered a group of athletes returning from an evening out on the town. The unwitting athletes helped the Palestinians and their bags full of weapons over the fence and into the village.

The eight men—Luttif "Issa" Afif, Yusuf "Tony" Nazzal, Mohammed Safady, Khalid Jawad, Adnan Al-Gashey, Jamal Al-Gashey, and Afif Ahmed Hamid—were members of Black September, an extreme faction of the Palestinian Liberation Organization (PLO). After scaling the fence, the guerrillas disguised their faces with black shoe polish or balaclavas and made their way to the Israeli compound at 31 Connollystrasse, which sat less than three hundred feet away.

The Israeli team's male athletes, coaches, and officials shared three apartments on the first floor of the building. The terrorists broke into the first apartment where the coaches slept and were confronted by Israeli wrestling coach Moshe Weinberg, who threw himself against the door in an attempt to keep the terrorists at bay. A burst of submachine gun fire blasted through the door and Weinberg was shot through the face.

"It was around four or five in the morning, and I heard the shots," said Frank Shorter, an American long-distance runner

The former Israeli dorms at 31 Connollystrasse, where the terrorist attack took place, are still in use.

Frank Shorter

who went on to win gold in the men's marathon in Munich. For several nights he had been sleeping on a mattress on the patio outside his team's apartment. "I thought to myself, *I've been out here for several days— that's not a door slamming. I would have heard a sound like that if it were part of the normal night sounds. That's a gun.*"

Badly wounded but still alive, Moshe Weinberg became the first hostage.

"Where are all the Israelis?" the terrorists asked him. "In which apartment?"

Weinberg led them past Apartment 2 to Apartment 3, which housed the biggest, strongest men on his team—the wrestlers and weightlifters. Despite their strength, the men in Apartment 3 were overpowered, and the Palestinians now had eleven Israeli hostages. At one

David Berger

Ze'ev Friedman

Yossef Gutfreund

Eliezer Halfin

Yossef Romano

Amitzur Shapira

Kehat Shorr

Mark Slavin

Andre Spitzer

Yakov Springer

Moshe Weinberg

Read more about these men and the legacy they left behind on page 74.

point, the gravely injured Moshe Weinberg and weightlifter Yossef Romano charged their captors. Weinberg knocked one Palestinian unconscious and slashed another with a knife. Romano was able to wound a third, but the Palestinians regained control, shooting the two Israelis and killing Weinberg. They tossed his body onto the sidewalk outside the building.

The terrorists led the rest of their hostages back to the coaches' apartment. The Israeli athletes in Apartment 2 eventually managed to escape from the building undetected.

AS THE WORLD WATCHED

"The Olympics of Serenity have become the one thing the Germans didn't want them to be–the Olympics of Terror."

—Reporter Jim McKay, broadcasting live from the ABC Studios in Munich

---

As the sun rose over the Olympic Village, word of the attack on the Israelis quickly spread to members of the media, the International Olympic Committee (IOC), and athletes in nearby buildings.

Neil Leifer

"A call came from my assistant," said photographer Neil Leifer, who was on staff with *Sports Illustrated* at the time. "She said, 'Something's going on, Neil. I think you ought to get dressed and head to the Olympic Village.' I said, 'What's happening?' She replied, 'Well, we don't know, but something is going on at the Israeli compound.'"

Peter Bonventre, a *Newsweek* journalist, recalls being in disbelief the first time he caught wind of the siege. Very early in the morning, he received a call from ABC sportscaster Howard Cosell.

"Howard said, 'My young friend, you listen closely to me. Arab terrorists have invaded the Israeli compound,'" recounted Bonventre. "And I'm thinking, 'Yeah right, Howard. Leave me alone, not

One of the eight Palestinian terrorist looks over the balcony of the Israeli Olympic compound.
(Photo: © Rich Clarkson / Rich Clarkson & Associates/Getty Images.)

funny.' And I hung up the phone. About three or four minutes later my phone rings again and it's [late sportswriter] Pete Axthelm. He said, 'Howard called me, and I don't think he's fooling around. We've got to get out there.'"

By 6:00 a.m. swarms of reporters, photographers, and camera crews amassed on the grassy banks about ninety yards from 31 Connollystrasse, some of them taking positions on nearby balconies. Outside of Munich, an estimated nine hundred million people around the world watched the first act of modern terrorism unfold on live television.

Sports journalist Jim McKay, who manned the anchor desk in the ABC Studios in Munich, became an iconic figure who narrated reportage of the attack for sixteen hours straight. Soon after going on the air, McKay said, "The Olympics of Serenity have become the one thing the Germans didn't want them to be—the Olympics of Terror."

From New Zealand's dorm next door to the Israeli compound, field hockey player Barry Maister could see the action unfold in scarily close proximity.

Barry Maister

"There was a lot of noise, a lot of shouting. I remember that morning pulling back the curtains and seeing a terrorist standing there with a gun," said Maister, now a member of the IOC. "Communication wasn't too good, and we didn't really know what was happening. Later we saw the tanks in the village; we saw the helicopters over-head. We knew this was a major act of terrorism, and we were in the middle of it."

"At some point that day, we actually saw the fellow with the hood and the AK-47 who was out there on the balcony," added Shorter. "We were so naïve. We just stood there and watched him, and he could have seen us and decided to shoot. It was the first time that anything like that had happened. Everyone was in shock."

As the crisis in the Israeli compound grew increasingly dire, dormitories in the vicinity of the Israeli compound were vacated, while other parts of the Olympic Village carried on as usual. IOC president Avery Brundage and members of the Olympic Committee learned of the attack early that morning but were anxious to see the Games continue. Morning competitions continued on schedule before thousands of cheering fans; athletes traded technical tips with their compatriots; others sunned and swam around the manmade lake that flanked the Village.

Issa addresses hostage negotiators outside of 31 Connollystrasse.
(Co Rentmeester/The LIFE Picture Collection/Getty Images)

"It was a beautiful day, and everybody was acting like nothing was going on. To this day, I'm not even sure they knew what was going on," said Bonventre. "Kids were throwing Frisbee, they were eating hamburgers, they were lolling on the hillside—and meanwhile Arab terrorists have captured eleven Israelis in their compound. It was a failure of imagination to grasp that this would happen at the Olympics, in Germany, and to Jewish athletes!"

Under increasing pressure, Brundage finally conceded to suspending the Games by mid-afternoon.

THE STANDOFF

After the first shots were fired in the Olympic Village, German police, along with local, state, federal, and Olympic officials, descended on the scene. From the terrace of the Israeli compound, the terrorists delivered their ransom letter detailing their demands:

Terrorist leader Luttif "Issa" Afif calls up to his second-in-command, Yusuf "Tony" Nazzal.
(Everett Collection Inc/ Alamy Stock Photo)

the hostages would be set free in exchange for the release of more than two hundred Palestinian prisoners from Israeli jails. If the demands weren't met, they committed to killing the Israelis, one by one.

The deadline was 9:00 a.m.

Israeli Prime Minister Golda Meir relayed to German authorities that under no circumstances would Jerusalem negotiate with terrorists or respond to blackmail.

German officials were at a loss as to how to handle a crisis of such magnitude. Hostage negotiators met with the Palestinians' leader, Luttif "Issa" Afif, on an upper terrace of the Israeli dorm. They succeeded in pushing the deadline back to noon, then to 1:00 p.m., then 3:00 p.m. Late in the afternoon, Hans-Dietrich Genscher, West Germany's federal minister of the interior, pleaded with Issa to consider the recent history of Jews on German soil, and offered himself as a hostage in exchange. The leader of the Palestinians refused. The terrorists wanted neither surrogate hostages nor large sums of money. Either their list of prisoners would be set free, or the hostages would die.

Around 5:00 p.m., German negotiators demanded to see the captive Israelis to ensure they were alive and well. Issa called up to a window on the terrace above. The curtain parted, the window opened, and there stood Andre Spitzer in a white tank top with his arms tied behind his back—a terrorist standing at his elbow. Andre spoke German and relayed information on behalf of the hostages to the crisis team below.

"He didn't have his glasses on. I found that so humiliating because I knew that he couldn't see without his glasses," noted his wife, Ankie, who had gone to visit her parents in Holland and watched the scene play out on television. "Afterward I asked what was said, and the officials said they asked him what is happening inside. And he said, 'Everybody is okay except for one.' And then they asked, 'Who is the one and what happened to him?' Andre was referring to Yossef Romano who had

Andre Spitzer is presented at the window to give a report to German authorities.
(United Archives GmbH / Alamy Stock Photo)

been shot, but before he had the chance to say that, you saw that he was hit with the butt of a rifle on his back, and then they just pushed him back into the room, and they closed the curtains and the windows. And that was really the last time that I saw my husband alive."

Olympic officials and German security forces had no idea what to do. They were completely unprepared, untrained, and unequipped.

"The Germans gave serious thought to storming the rooms where the Israelis were being held," said Leifer. "The element of surprise being important, they dressed in track suits. One was dressed in blue, another in red, all carrying automatic weapons."

Cameras broadcasted live as police in tracksuits stood on the roof of the Israeli building, making their way down the terraces to where the hostages were

Andre Spitzer, fluent in German, relays information on behalf of the hostages to the crisis team on the ground below. (Everett Collection Inc / Alamy Stock Photo)

Armed police officers dressed in track suits attempt a raid on the Israeli compound.
(Photo by Guido Cegani; Mario De Biasi; Sergio Del Grande; Giorgio Lotti; Walter Mori; Giuseppe Pino/Mondadori Portfolio via Getty Images)

being held. Their plan was to infiltrate the building through the ventilation system and take the terrorists by surprise. The entire world watched the operation in progress—including the terrorists, who were also watching television inside the dorm. When police realized their mistake, they called off the operation and tried to calm the Palestinians.

After several hours of tense negotiations, the Palestinians grew weary and refused to postpone their demands any longer. Issa demanded a jet to fly them to Cairo, Egypt, where negotiations could continue on Arab ground.

"Why Egypt? Because these Israelis would arrive to the Arab countries, and they would be arrested as citizens of an enemy country," explained Rael Othman, journalist and founder of Ma'an News Agency, who provided the Palestinian perspective for the *Munich '72 and Beyond* documentary. "After that, the job of the fighters would be finished."

Around 10:00 p.m., a gray, German army bus arrived in the garage below the Israeli compound and took the terrorists and their hostages through a tunnel to a strip of lawn where two helicopters waited to ferry them to Fürstenfeldbruck, a seldom-used German Air Force base about fifteen miles west of the Olympic site. A third helicopter transported German authorities and Zvi Zamir, the director of Mossad, Israel's intelligence agency, who had arrived earlier in the evening.

"A bunch of us who were about ninety yards from the entrance to the Israeli compound saw the bus arrive, and we could barely make out shadows of people being led onto the bus," remembered Bonventre. "We figured it must be the Israeli athletes. Where were they taking them? Those of us in the Village had really no idea what was going on. There were no cellphones or Internet. It was hard to get any kind of information about what was happening."

"I remember my mother saying 'that's a good sign when all the hostages are being taken out,'" recounted Ankie. "I said, 'No, it's not a good sign.' All the time they are in the Olympic Village and the focus of the world, they have a chance. If they're taken to some small, way-out airfield, that's the end of them. What the Germans wanted was to just continue with their fun Games. They wanted to take the drama out of the Olympic Village so that life could go on. That was, for me, a very bad moment when I saw them being taken out."

Athletes, journalists, and other witnesses around the Olympic Village remember with startling clarity the helicopters' flashing lights and the thick, pulsing of their rotors as they lifted off their makeshift

A gray German bus arrives to escort the terrorists and hostages to waiting helicopters.
(Raymond Depardon/Magnum Photos)

launch pad and flew toward Fürstenfeldbruck. The Germans had no intention of actually letting the terrorists leave with the hostages to a country hostile to Israel. Their plan instead was to ambush them at the airport, but a ripple of egregious errors was already underway before the helicopters even arrived.

"Nobody foresaw such an attack," said Hans-Jochen Vogel, former mayor of Munich, who led the campaign to host the Olympics.

No one, that is, but police psychologist Georg Sieber.

In advance of the Munich Games, Dr. Sieber, who was thirty-nine at the time, was hired by Olympic organizers to draft hypothetical crisis situations so that security measures could be fashioned accordingly. Dr. Sieber was well versed in the extremist organizations of the day, including the Irish Republican Army, the Palestinian Liberation Organization (PLO), and West German's Red Army Faction. He identified twenty-six possible scenarios, including hijacked planes, remote-controlled bombs, kidnappers and hostages, all written out to the last catastrophic detail and focusing most heavily on harm that could come to the Olympic Village.

His situation No. 21 turned out to be chilling in its prophetic accuracy.

Dr. Sieber predicted that at five o'clock one morning, a dozen armed Palestinians would scale a fence at the Olympic Village and break into the dormitory that housed the Israeli delegation. In a display of power, they would kill a hostage or two, and then demand the release of prisoners held in Israeli jails and a plane to fly to an Arab capital.[8]

The Olympic organizers balked at the list of apocalyptic threats Dr. Sieber had imagined. If they embraced these possibilities, there would be no way to avoid militarizing the entire Olympic complex or canceling the Games entirely. They requested that Dr. Sieber return with less severe scenarios more in keeping with the Happy Games they intended to hold.

Hours into the hostage crisis on September 5, Dr. Sieber joined the crisis team near the site of the siege. At one point, he was told that his help was no longer needed. "This is no longer a psychological matter," said Munich police chief Manfred Schreiber, "but a political one."[9]

From the start of the operation, Dr. Sieber feared the worst. He resigned his post shortly thereafter.[10]

"Munich was an unspeakable catastrophe because it didn't have to happen," said sportswriter Jeremy Schaap. "And what happened changed everything, not just for security at the Olympics, but for all big sports events everywhere. When you walk into an arena now, you can't help but notice the layers of security that are present—all this traces back to Munich. Nobody wants to have another Munich on their hands."

The events in Munich permanently altered attitudes and approaches to security in every subsequent Olympics. Security costs, which were around $2 million for Munich, soared to $100 million for the 1976 Summer Olympics in Montreal. After 9/11, the security bill for the 2002 Winter Olympics in Salt Lake City hit more than $500 million. Security costs continue to hover between $1 billion and $2 billion at contemporary Games.

"I doubt the White House is as secure as the Olympic Village is now, and that's 100 percent because of what happened in Munich," said photographer Neil Leifer.

CHAPTER 2: FAILURE AT FÜRSTENFELDBRUCK

"The latest word we get from the airport is that, quote, 'All hell has broken loose out there,' that there's still shooting going on, there's report of a burning helicopter. All seems to be confusion; nothing is nailed down. We have no idea what's happened to the hostages."

–Reporter Jim McKay, broadcasting live from the ABC Studios in Munich

WAITING AT THE Fürstenfeldbruck air base was a Lufthansa Boeing 727. Undercover police officers clad in flight crew uniforms were positioned inside the jet to take out the terrorists upon arrival. Five snipers had taken their positions—three on the roof of the main tower and two more on the ground. Fifty uniformed policemen stood guard outside the entrance gates. The crisis team set up inside the control tower.

Among the crisis team was the head of Israeli intelligence, Zvi Zamir, but he was authorized only as an observer. In his official report to Israeli Defense Secretary Moshe Dayan and Prime Minister Golda Meir, Zamir noted that his first impression was that the operation was going well.

"At this point, we were very encouraged," he wrote. "The terrorists had complete trust in the Germans."

Plans for the ambush started to crumble, however, before the helicopters had landed. Knowing the terrorists had hand grenades, the undercover crew on the plane voted to abandon what they viewed as a suicide mission. None of the snipers had rifles with telescopic sights, nor night vision goggles, nor bulletproof vests or helmets. The snipers weren't made aware of where exactly the helicopters would land, and once they did,

Investigators inspect the aftermath of the fight at Fürstenfeldbruck, including one of the helicopters destroyed by a grenade. *(Photo by Bettmann Archive/Getty Images)*

the two snipers across the tarmac ended up directly in the line of fire of those on the rooftops. And none of the operatives—the snipers or the crew who aborted their mission—had walkie-talkies to communicate with each other about such crucial changes to the operation.

CHAOS AT FÜRSTENFELDBRUCK

When the terrorists and their hostages arrived at the airfield, the two Palestinian leaders, Issa and Tony, went to inspect the jet. Upon seeing an empty plane,

they knew they'd been tricked.

"The mistake was that they went alone without taking the hostages with them—from the Palestinian point of view," said Palestinian journalist Rael Othman. "So on their way back, the German snipers killed them."

Zamir recalled the events differently. "They shot one terrorist and killed him," he reported. "They shot the second. He fired afterwards."

During the fight at Fürstenfeldbruck, a terrorist threw a grenade into one of the helicopters.
(dpa picture alliance / Alamy Stock Photo)

Though one terrorist was killed immediately en route back to the helicopters, the other survived long enough to continue fighting. The terrorists shot out the lights around the base to hide their positions. The airfield was now cloaked in darkness. Zamir reported one disillusionment after another. The German police snipers shooting with pistols were entirely outgunned by the terrorists' semiautomatic weapons. There were eight terrorists instead of the expected five. There was no reinforcement. The armored vehicles were blocked by hordes of would-be spectators and

In this forensics photo, circles and arrows indicate bullet holes in one of the helicopters.
(Photo by Rolls Press/Popperfoto/Getty Images)

members of the media who thronged the roads outside of the airfield. The breakdown in communications and logistics allowed the remaining terrorists to hold in check four hundred German police officers.

Zamir's most damning statement of the German effort: "They did not make the minimal effort to save lives."

In the pitch black of night, the Israeli hostages might have been able to escape the helicopters, but they were tied fast to their seats. Before being shot down, one of the terrorists strafed the Israelis inside one helicopter, and then tossed a grenade into the cockpit. The remaining hostages in the second helicopter were also shot dead.

Back at the ABC broadcast center, Jim McKay reported, "The latest word we get from the airport is that, quote, 'All hell has broken loose out there,' that there's still shooting going on, there's report of a burning helicopter. All seems to be confusion; nothing is nailed down. We have no idea what's happened to the hostages."

"Nobody knew what was going on," said Ankie Spitzer. "You could only hear on television the firing of the rifles. Then at one point there was a huge explosion, and you could see flames when one of the helicopters was set alight. They threw a hand grenade in there. Nobody could say what was happening. I wondered, *What is going on? Who is fighting whom there?*"

"OUR WORST FEARS HAVE BEEN REALIZED."

Just before midnight, Conrad Ahlers, spokesman for the German government,

appeared on McKay's ongoing broadcast to update viewers about the actions at Fürstenfeldbruck.

"I'm very glad that, as far as we can see now, this police action was successful," he told McKay. "I mean, if all comes out as we hope, I think it will be forgotten after a few weeks."

Though the origin of such a cruel falsehood is unclear, the message took flight. Newspaper headlines around the world declared the hostages free and the terrorists dead.

"Pandemonium broke out in my house," said Ankie. "My father opened a champagne bottle, and then everybody was starting to call, and kiss, and I said, 'No. I am not convinced of anything until I hear Andre.' I knew that even if he was exhausted or maybe even wounded, the first thing he would do is call me. 'Until he calls,' I told them, 'I cannot celebrate.' And so we waited."

Not long after Ahlers's late night

ABC sportscaster Jim McKay reported live from Munich throughout the crisis.
(ABC Photo Archives/ABC via Getty Images)

pronouncement that all was well, the backtracking began.

"Originally, they said the hostages were safe; now that has been changed," said McKay in his broadcast. "An Olympic spokesman said, 'We are afraid the information given so far is too optimistic.'"

"I called the head of the Israeli delega-

tion [Shmuel Lalkin] at the Olympic Village," said Ankie. "I asked him, 'Where is everybody? Why doesn't Andre call?' He said, 'I don't know, but they said maybe some of them are wounded, so wait patiently.' At one o'clock in the morning I called, at one thirty, and at two o'clock, and at two thirty. Every time the story became worse; maybe some of them were killed. Nobody knew what was going on. At three o'clock I called again and then afterward, I didn't have to call because Jim McKay came on."

"I remember this chilling moment vividly," said Steven Ungerleider, one of the producers of *Munich '72 and Beyond.* "I had hoped to attend the 1972 Summer Games in Munich, but when my father died suddenly, I left my doctoral studies at the University of Oregon to be with my mother in New York. Forty-five years later, I can still remember where I was sitting when ABC News broke the story. As the hostage crisis played out, we were glued to the television in complete disbelief and hanging onto McKay's every word. I was in shock."

At 3:24 a.m. Munich time, McKay leaned toward his colleagues and said, "When I was a kid, my father used to say that our greatest hopes and our worst fears are seldom realized. But tonight, our worst fears have been realized."

He then turned toward the camera and addressed the watching world. "They've now said that there were eleven hostages. Two were killed in their rooms yesterday morning. Nine were killed at the airport tonight. They're all gone."

The Israeli hostages, along with German policeman Anton Fliegerbauer, were killed in the firefight at Fürstenfeldbruck airport.

They're all gone.

"I don't think I was twenty yards from him when he said that," said Peter Bonventre. "And to this day, I think those were the saddest words I've ever heard spoken on any event that I ever covered. That's for sure. That was a shock to the system. You felt it all over."

The dramatic reversal sent people around the world reeling.

"Even today, this violent death of the eleven Israeli athletes and the Bavarian police officer was a shock," said Ludwig Spaenle, minister of education and culture in Bavaria, who was eleven years old at the time of the Munich Games. "It was

Ludwig Spaenle

a deep shock for our family, for the whole city of Munich, and all of Germany. Because my family lived nearby, it was as if an uncle was killed—something personal like that."

Igal Carmi

"There was a certain time that we were sure that the rescue operation was successful," said Igal Carmi, who was elected president of the Israel Olympic Committee in 2013, who was a sixteen-

year-old high school student at the time of the attack. "For an hour everyone in Israel was very happy. When the sad part of the story came, it was a very dramatic moment for everybody. Even as a kid, I remember my parents and neighbors talking about this big event that caught everyone in Israel."

"THE GAMES MUST GO ON."

On Wednesday, September 6, while German forensics teams canvassed the airfield in the morning light, more than eighty thousand people filed into the Olympic Stadium for a memorial service to honor the slain athletes. The Olympic flag and the flags of the nations flew at half-mast—except for the Arab countries, which refused the tribute.

The Israeli delegation sat ahead of their fellow Olympians in the center field, eleven empty seats among them. The mourners in attendance included heads of state, star Olympians, and athletes from around the world. Many in the devastated crowd wept openly.

"We knew of acts of terrorism, but not in this context," said Bonventre. "Not coming in for no reason and taking eleven innocent athletes' lives."

"It was the first time, outside the borders of Israel, that a terror attack took place, and against purely civilians that didn't do anything to anyone," noted Noam Schiller. "That was a shock."

IOC president Avery Brundage addressed the mourners: "Every civilized person recoils in horror at the barbarous criminal intrusion of terrorists into peaceful Olympic precincts. We mourn our Israeli friends—victims of this brutal assault."

At the end of his speech, Brundage made his now infamous declaration: "The Games must go on!" he said. "We declare today a day of mourning and will continue all the events one day later than originally scheduled."

The decision evoked strong reactions from athletes and spectators alike.

"How can the games go on after a tragedy like this? We thought it was terrible and disgusting and disrespectful and typical of what a crusty old Avery Brundage would do," said Bonventre.

"There aren't many moments in which a great organization has an opportunity to tell the world what it stands for and demonstrate that with action," said Jeremy Schaap. "The Olympic movement had that opportunity in '72. There were many ways in which it could have said, 'This is an unspeakable tragedy; we're shutting down the Games.' Whatever it might have been, it was botched. Brundage botched it."

Protestors marched against the decision. People horrified by the attack on the Israelis held rallies and demanded the Games be shut down—but to no avail.

"The whole city discussed this, 'Should the Games be stopped or should it go on?'" said Spaenle. "It was a very intensive, emotional debate for a boy only eleven-years-old. Then at the memorial service,

I remember the famous sentence, 'The Games must go on!' I remember where I was standing and this emotional wave going around the stadium. It was the right thing to do."

"I'm not making a judgment, but many, if not most, athletes were happy the Games went on. This was a one-shot thing," admitted Bonventre.

"We thought we'd hear that this was the end of the Olympic Games," said Barry Maister, whose New Zealand field hockey team had one game left on the schedule. "How can the Games possibly advance beyond this point? How can you bring normality and sanity back to the situation? The notion that the Games will go on and terrorism will not prevail was unbelievably powerful and very, very emotional."

Speaking of his running teammates, Frank Shorter said, "After the attack, our thought initially, to a person, was, 'That's it, we're going home.' No one complained. People had died; nothing

is that important. But we were in shock. My feeling when they decided to continue the Olympics was yes, that's what you have to do. It very quickly dawned on me that we all had to go forward."

For the families of the victims, the decision to go forward turned a blind eye to what happened.

Alex Springer

"It was a shock for us, how the world could continue like nothing had happened," recalled Alex Springer, son of Israeli weightlifting coach Yakov Springer, who was sixteen when his dad was killed. "It was another trauma for us, besides the loss of my father and the sportsmen. How can the world continue regular life and the Games and everything like nothing had happened? It wasn't acceptable. It was terrible."

Ankie Spitzer returned to Munich from Holland in time to make the memorial service at the Olympic Stadium, and was stunned to see life around her continuing as if it were just another normal, sunny day.

"It was surrealistic," she said. "On the right and on the left I'm looking, and people are training on the athletic field there. I still remember thinking, 'Eleven people were murdered! And everybody is still going on with the Olympics.'"

At the time, proceeding with the Munich Games seemed grossly inappropriate. The general consensus in the years since, however, is that terrorism shouldn't be allowed to disrupt everyday life.

"Forty-plus years later, you never give in. You keep it going, right? If they had stopped the Games, the terrorists would have won," said Bonventre. "Back then, we didn't think that way because it was so new to us. Today, I don't think there would be any question—you would not stop the Games; you would keep going."

THE AFTERMATH

The Games of the Twentieth Olympiad resumed around 4:30 p.m. that afternoon—only twenty-four hours since they were first suspended, and thirty-four hours since the start of the crisis.

After the memorial ceremony, members of the organizing committee asked the surviving members of the Israeli team to go back to the rooms and gather the victims' belongings.

"So I said, 'Okay, I'll pick up Andre's stuff,'" said Ankie, "and they said, 'No, no, no, you cannot go there because in his room they were kept hostage, and that's where they killed Yossef Romano.' And I said, 'Yes, but I will go there. I want to see the place where my husband spent the last hours of his life.' I went with one of his fencing students, also an Olympic athlete who survived because he was in the room next door."

Ankie was determined to enter 31 Connollystrasse and the apartment where her husband had been held hostage.

Ankie Spitzer surveys the room in which the Israeli athletes were held and two were killed.
(Popperfoto/Getty Images)

"I went back to the apartment and opened the door. There was a staircase, and I had to go up because it was on the second floor. And the blood was coming down from where they had shot Romano," said Ankie. "I said, 'If it already looks like this here, what will it look like in the room?' Andre's student stood next to me and said, 'Please don't go up, please don't go up.' I said, 'I must see what happened there.' And I went up to the room, and I stood there, and I cannot even describe the chaos that was in that room."

The hostages had been tied by their hands and legs to the tables and beds. There were four large holes in the wall from rifle shots. Where Yossef Romano was shot, there was blood pooling on the floor. There

A glimpse of the chaos inside the room in which the Israeli athletes were held hostage.

were food cartons and trash scattered everywhere. And the hostages hadn't been allowed to go to the bathroom.

"It was huge chaos," said Ankie. "I stood there and said, 'If somebody did this to my peace-loving husband—who was only filled with being part of the Olympic idea and who never did anything wrong to anyone—I'm not going to shut up for the rest of my life. I'm going to remind people what happened there so this will never, ever happen again, because I owe it to him and to his teammates.'

"Justice has to be done for these people, because they didn't come with guns. They were not on the battlefield. They came to the peaceful, joyful, brotherhood Games in Munich, and this is what happened to them. This is how they spent their last hours—in fear, being humiliated.

"I'm not going home and accepting that this is what happened to me. Somebody is going to tell me exactly how it happened and why it happened. Somebody is going to pay the price for this—some-body is going to take responsibility for what happened to these people in the middle of the Olympic Village."

Ankie would continue that quest—for the next forty-three years.

The surviving members of the Israeli team were flown home, along with the ten caskets of their fallen teammates. President Nixon sent a US Air Force jet to fly David Berger's remains home to his parents in Ohio.

"This is how they spend their last hours—in fear, being humiliated. Somebody is going to take responsibility for what happened to these people in the middle of the Olympic Village."

—Ankie Spitzer, widow of Israeli fencing coach Andre Spitzer

THE PALESTINIAN PERSPECTIVE

During filming for the *Munich '72 and Beyond*, we asked journalists Rael Othman and Ziad Zayyad to offer the Palestinian point of view regarding the events of September 5.

Rael Othman

Ziad Zayyad

"One of the reasons why they did it," said Othman, "is to introduce the Palestinian case, issue, problems, to the world."

"When this took place, the international community and the world did not pay attention, unfortunately, to the Palestinian case, and their demands to live in freedom and independently, but after that event, most of the international community paid attention," added Zayyad.

"We didn't release the prisoners, but

we managed all of our goals that we wanted from the Munich activity. This is what Abu Iyad [aka Salah Mesbah Khalaf, deputy chief and head of intelligence for the PLO] himself said, and this is the highest person responsible for this activity."

According to Zayyad, the Palestinians never wanted to use force or violence as a tool just for the sake of using it. Their strategy was to take advantage of this global platform to garner support for their movement using clear demands and conditions that would lead to a solution.

"All of the struggles since 1965 till today has been taking place in order to get freedom for our people," he said.

Othman reiterated that sentiment. "There was a very high restriction to the Palestinians not to be violent, not to kill any of the hostages. Killing was the last thing that they can do."

We learned, in a shocking moment with

Ankie, how at odds that interpretation of history was with evidence she later revealed.

LUFTHANSA FLIGHT 615

Five of the Palestinian terrorists died in the firefight at Fürstenfeldbruck. Their remains were sent to Libya, where they were embraced as martyrs and given a hero's funeral. The three who survived, Mohammed Safady, Adnan Al-Gashey, and Jamal Al-Gashey,[11] were taken into custody, but they never stood trial.

On October 29, 1972, Lufthansa flight 615 from Syria en route to Germany was hijacked over the Mediterranean Sea by two members of Black September. They demanded the release of the three terrorists held in Munich in exchange for the safe release of the plane and its passengers and crew.

The speedy and efficient response of West German chancellor Willy Brandt raised doubts about the authenticity of this attack: the prisoners were located from three separate jails and delivered for transport within hours.[12] Also suspicious was the fact that the Lufthansa flight had only about a dozen passengers—all of them men.[13] That the hijacking was likely a set-up to allow Germany to remove the terrorists and reduce the threat of further attacks on German soil has since been supported by numerous German, Israeli, and Palestinian intelligence sources.[14]

The three newly released terrorists received the same hero's welcome in Libya as had their five dead compatriots.

Within days of the murders in Munich, Israel began a fierce retaliation that included widespread airstrikes, military ground offensives, and a covert assassination protocol called Operation Wrath of God aimed at not only the surviving terrorists, but also leaders of Black September who were believed to have organized and instigated the attacks.

Only one of the original eight Palestinian terrorists is still alive as of this writing—Jamal Al-Gashey, who is presumed to be in hiding in North Africa with his wife and children.

PART 2

THE FIGHT FOR JUSTICE

CHAPTER 3

THE COVER-UP

"There is so much to tell, but it was comfortable for them to cover up all those very difficult facts."

–Mika Slavin, sister of slain Israeli Olympic wrestler Mark Slavin

AFTER THE FALLOUT at Fürstenfeldbruck, the West German government founded a counterterrorism and special operations unit in the federal police force to ensure a more effective response to any potential future crises. Though this development acknowledged their lack of readiness for extremist violence, German authorities offered no formal admission of culpability to the families of the Israeli athletes who died in Munich.

The stunned survivors of the Israeli Olympic delegation arrived at Lod Airport just outside Tel Aviv on the morning of September 7. The team was met by nearly five thousand people, among whom were their slain comrades' family members, utterly racked by grief.

"The first time I met everyone—all the families—was when they all arrived at the airport," said Ilana Romano, widow of weightlifter Yossef Romano. "It was the first time we all knew who was murdered."

Following the Munich massacre, the family members of the murdered athletes gained in each other an extended family born of this shared trauma.

"We have found strength in each other," said Michal Shahar, daughter of victim Kehat Shorr, the shooting coach and senior member of the Israeli Olympic delegation in Munich. "We call ourselves the family of the eleven. There are very strong heart strings between us. Ankie and Ilana, they are the ones who have done

On September 7, five thousand mourners surround ten coffins during a mass open-air funeral on an airport runway.

the most, but we know when we are called to the flag—a Hebrew expression—everyone is coming."

A STRUGGLE FOR TRUTH AND JUSTICE

In the midst of their profound pain, widows Ilana Romano and Ankie Spitzer

Michal Sharar

found solace and strength in a burgeoning sense of sisterhood. Not long after their husbands' funerals, the two began spearheading the fight on behalf of the victims' survivors to find out what happened in Munich. Galvanized into action, Ankie and Ilana spent the next two decades knocking on every door in every possible venue to seek answers, but their requests for the results of the investigation were repeatedly denied.

"The German government kept saying to me, 'We don't have any information,'" said Ankie. "Now, I'm from Holland, and I know the German mentality. Everything is documented—every word. Everything is organized. I said, 'It cannot be that you don't have this information. Eight terrorists came in and killed eleven Israelis, and that's it?' They were lying—the Bavarian government, the federal government—everyone was lying about the fact that they didn't have the information."

In early 1992, nearly twenty years after the massacre, Ankie had her first major breakthrough. During an interview on

the German television station ZDF, she discussed the impending anniversary and her ongoing struggle for information on how her husband, Andre, had died at the Munich Olympics.

"After I got back to Israel," said Ankie, "somebody from the archives of the Bavarian court called and said, 'Look, you don't know me, but I can tell you that you are absolutely right—there are thousands of documents they haven't given to you.' So I asked him for proof."

Proof arrived in the form of eighty sample pages from the ballistic and pathological reports and other investigative findings that confirmed long-held assumptions about German incompetence in the failed rescue attempt. Also included in the envelope was an index of nearly four thousand files from the Munich investigation—proof that the Bavarian government had, in fact, been lying to Ankie all along.

Armed with evidence of the massive cover-up, Ankie contacted the minister of foreign affairs in Germany.

Ilana Romano and Anke Spitzer *(Jack Guez /AFP/Getty Images)*

"I didn't let him know that I had only eighty pages," she explained. "I told him, 'I have most of the material; now I want all of it.' He said, 'Why don't you take what you have and show it to the German ambassador in Tel Aviv, and he can see what else you need.' And I said, 'No. You don't think I was born yesterday, right? I'm not going to show anybody anything. I just want everything.'"

Ankie's claims unleashed a political firestorm in Germany, including intense discussions in the German parliament and heated exchanges between the federal and Bavarian authorities about what files were or weren't housed in the Bavarian archives. Two months later, at the end of August in 1992, German officials finally invited Ankie Spitzer and the other survivors to the archives in Munich. Their attorney, Pinchas Zeltzer, made the trip on the families' behalf.

While preparing to film the *Munich '72 and Beyond* documentary, Ulich and

Ungerleider conducted extensive research into the terrorist siege and subsequent massacre. What we learned from Ankie proved gruesome and unnerving. During our interviews with her, Ankie shared details about what she saw in those files first discovered back in 1992.

"There were three walls full of dossiers of files, and nine hundred forensic pictures," Ankie said. "Ilana and I are the only ones of the families who saw these pictures. Of course, we told the families that everybody is allowed to see them, but we advised them not to look, because I cannot even—most of the athletes were burned. I cannot even start explaining what this looked like."

Then she said, "I think you all should know that this was not just a hostage story and horrific murder in the Olympic Village—there was torture."

There were about seven of us in that hotel room in Tel Aviv for the filming, and all of us froze.

"This is something I've lived with for all my life," she said, "and I just need to get it off my chest. I need to get it out of my being from now on."

After all these years in the Olympic movement, we thought we knew the whole story of the Munich massacre, but Ankie's interview proved we didn't know the worst of it. For twenty years, Ankie and Ilana had been guarding from the public the grisly truth revealed in those forensic photos.

"Our lawyer pulled me aside and said, 'Look, there are pictures that I don't want Ilana to see.' He showed me the pictures. I said, 'If it were my husband, I would want to see that. I know her. We're friends—we'll get through this. But I think she should see it, or at least ask her.' So he did, and she looked at me, and I said, 'You have to see it or else you cannot say it.' And so we all saw what happened to him."

We had the opportunity to view these horrible photographs during our interview with Ankie. These pictures, which were very hard to take and left us completely shaken, revealed details far crueler and more painful than anyone had been led to believe. Yossef Romano did not die immediately after being shot. As he lay on the floor, the Palestinians castrated him and left him to bleed to death in front of his teammates. The terrorists abused and humiliated Romano in ways not fit to print.

"It was brutal what they did to him," Ilana later said, in reference to what Ankie had revealed.

Other hostages were beaten and tortured and sustained serious injuries like broken bones.

"I said, 'Ankie, I cannot show these photographs to the families. I'm just unable.' They were very hard photos, unbearable to see," added Ilana.

"My dad saw the very difficult pictures of what happened in this room where they were held," said Mika Slavin, the

Ilana Romano

Mika Slavin

youngest sister of wrestler Mark Slavin. "When I used to ask him, 'What did you see in those pictures?', it's the first time that I saw him crying. He told me, 'Promise me that you will never ask to see those pictures.'"

The proof of torture confirmed what many had suspected: The terrorists came prepared to maim and destroy. After we saw the forensic evidence, we reached out to journalists Ziad Zayyad and Raed Othman, who had provided commentary on the events from the Palestinian point of view. Zayyad wrote back saying, "We were not aware of these actions. We don't condone violence. This was unacceptable." We received no reply from Othman.

The forensic pictures and investigative reports unearthed in 1992 shed a harsh light on both the terrorists' actions and those of the German authorities tasked with protecting the hostages. Ankie and the surviving relatives wanted Germany held accountable for what they considered criminal negligence, as demonstrated in the reports.

"We got the pictures and the four thousand files, which is only a very, very small part of what is there—there is much more. And with these files, we went to work," stated Ankie. "We sued the German government, the city of Munich, and the State of Bavaria. After eight years in the court system, which cost us millions that we didn't have, they threw us out on account of the statute of limitations. For me, that was one of the most important things to get justice done."

In September of 2002, a few days after the thirtieth anniversary of the Munich massacre, Germany paid the victims' families a settlement of about three million euros, which was intended more as a humanitarian gesture than any admission of responsibility.

In 2012, around the fortieth anniversary, Israel State Archives released dozens of previously classified documents related to the attacks, including the eyewitness report by Mossad chief Zvi Zamir of the botched rescue attempt, which held numerous revelations about the events on September 5.

"When we went to the fortieth anniversary memorial service at Fürstenfeldbruck airport," said Ilana Romano. "Mika Slavin came up to me, and it was the first time she asked what happened to her brother. And so I told her. But until then, no one else knew what we knew."

"I didn't even know if he was in this helicopter or the other helicopter, whether he got shot, or exploded, I didn't know," said Mika Slavin. "It was facts the Germans hid from us. Even Israel—there is so much to tell, but it was comfortable for them to cover up all those very difficult facts. It's very frustrating."

Despite the decades-long cover-up by both nations, the widows of the Israeli athletes had remained convinced all along that the truth was there and would be revealed.

"Now, forty years afterward, we have a different German government, a different mentality—not the same guys that were there in the early '70s," said Ankie. "They are from a different generation, and they heard our plea, and they have opened again all the archives. I have a team of German lawyers roaming around Germany to gather the enormous amount of information.

"We knew it was not a simple case of eight Palestinians coming to kill eleven Israelis. It was much more complicated. Slowly we are finding out just how complicated it was, who was involved, and what happened. And we are overwhelmed by all the new information. So if you think that I can say, 'Let me go home. Let me go finish this whole thing.' No. I owe it not only to these eleven athletes, but also to my daughter, and to the next generation. We are not going home until we get the full truth, and the people who are responsible take full responsibility."

A MOMENT OF SILENCE

Despite their progress in tracking down the truth, one very important goal still eluded the relatives of the murdered athletes—official recognition from the International Olympic Committee (IOC). The request seemed simple: have a moment of silence during an Opening Ceremony to remember the fallen sportsmen, and to inspire young athletes to protect each other. After the Munich Games, Ankie, Ilana, and other survivors fought continuously for that moment of silence at each subsequent Olympics, but were met with excuse after excuse.

Israel joins the Parade of Nations at the Opening Ceremony of the 2012 London Olympics.
(Leon Neal /AFP/Getty Images)

"I went with Ilana and Ankie, the three of us to the Summer Olympics in Montreal in '76," said Michal Shahar. "This was the first time that we tried to make a change, a moment of silence. We met with every journalist there, the mayor of the city, Jewish community, but as you know, nothing happened. From then on, every four years—Ankie and Ilana even more than I—met with everyone possible. We don't understand why they don't do it. There's not even a word for how frustrated we are."

"First, they accused me of bringing politics into the Olympics," said Ankie. "The IOC told us very clearly: 'There are twenty-one Arab delegations that will leave if we say something about the Israeli athletes.' I said, 'If you don't want to say that they were Israelis, or Jews, then just say that eleven athletes who were part of the Olympic family were tortured and brutally murdered in the Olympic Village. Why don't you want to recognize what happened?'

"In Athens in 2004, the tune changed again. They said, 'It is too early.' I said, 'It's too early? What, do you want me to come with a cane or being pushed in a wheelchair, and then finally you are going to do it? What is the difficulty? Why is it so hard? Is it because they're from Israel? Is that the reason?'"

Ankie and Ilana started a petition on Change.org for a minute of silence at the 2012 London Olympics that received more than 111,500 signatures. Heads of state such as US president Barack Obama and Australian prime minister Julia Gillard openly promoted the initiative. Despite widespread support, the IOC remained obstinate.

"We went to London, and they said, 'It is not appropriate to remember something so sad at the glorious, fun opening ceremony,'" Ankie said.

The 2012 Summer Olympics in London took place a little more than a month before the fortieth anniversary of the Munich massacre. Those of us with Global Sports Development were also in attendance, and we remember how the IOC caved to anti-Israel sentiment in the Middle East. We found it to be an unfair political calculation that deeply harmed the relatives of the murdered athletes.

If the IOC's refusal wasn't bad enough, what happened at the Opening Ceremony just added insult to injury.

"Ladies and gentlemen," the announcer said, "please pause to respect our memorial wall for friends and family of those in the stadium that cannot be here tonight. Thank you."

On July 7, 2005—the day after London won its bid for the 2012 Summer Olympics—the Underground was bombed by Islamic extremists. The Opening Ceremony in 2012 honored those lost in the terrorist attack.

"They mentioned, rightly so, the fifty-two people that were killed in the terrorist attack in the Metro, and the victims of the Second World War—all kinds of peo-ple," noted Ankie. "But this was not appropriate, even though it happened *at the Olympics.* I'm so fed up with the lame excuses. Is it only because they came from Israel? Then say it so I understand, because until now I don't understand you at all."

"I have to conclude that if the fallen Olympians had been from a less controversial country in the Olympic movement, more would have been done," noted Jeremy Schaap. "I think there was a reluctance to single out Israel, which suffered this unique tragedy at the Games, and I thought it was shameful. There should have been a moment of silence in the stadium."

For these dedicated families, the fight for just sixty seconds of recognition has been a lifelong endeavor.

"When I began, I say, okay, two years, four years, one Olympics in Montreal, and the second, and a third, and now, ten," said Ilana. "I lost all my life. I put Ilana inside. I forgot about Ilana."

Ilana's daughter Oshat Romano Kandell was not yet seven years old when her father was shot and mutilated on the floor of the Israeli apartment at 31 Connollystrasse.

Oshat Romano Kandell

"It was so difficult to wake up every morning with the thought that you have to fight for the documents or fight in court or fight for a moment of silence and not winning all these years," Oshat said. "We couldn't understand how the IOC could be so cruel. How could they not understand that these eleven athletes deserved the memorial in the place where they were murdered? If the IOC had been more cooperative, it would have made it much easier, because it seemed that they didn't care about these Israelis. Their lives weren't precious like they were to us."

"It's like the B'nai Yisrael were walking in the desert for forty years before Moses gave them Israel," said Mika, "and now we're forty-three years after, and still nothing. It's not fair."

At each of the Olympic Games since Munich, Israeli representatives hosted private memorial services, often with IOC members in attendance. But the IOC continued to refuse any memorial to be officially sanctioned as part of the Olympics themselves. Their stance held firm for more than four decades, but a new generation of leaders in the IOC would, in time, answer the survivors' cries for remembrance.

A MOMENT OF GLORY

Since that dark day in Munich, the words Israeli and Olympics in the same sentence rarely connoted anything but tragedy—until Yael Arad made her debut at the 1992 Summer Games in Barcelona, Spain.

Just prior to the twentieth anniversary of the Munich massacre, Arad, a judo athlete, became the first Israeli Olympic medalist in the history of her people.

"I was five when the massacre occurred, and growing up as a girl athlete in Israel, it was part of our Olympic tradition," said Arad, who was interviewed during the filming of *Munich '72 and Beyond.* "This massacre took almost the whole generation of Israeli Olympic athletes. Even the ones who survived—the guys in the second room, the shooters and others who hid from the terrorists—they couldn't go on. They were lost. It makes you terrified to go on competing later when your friends or coaches were killed in this kind of mas-

Yael Arad celebrates winning the Judo semifinals at the 1992 Barcelona Games.
(Phil O'Brien/EMPICS/Getty Images)

sacre. For me, part of the younger generation of Israeli athletes, I saw it and felt it."

After completing her military service, Arad left Israel to find expert judo training in Europe and Japan. She competed in the World Judo Championships, won medals in several European Championships, and steadily rose to the top ranks of judokas.

YAEL ARAD

Before leaving for Barcelona, Arad arranged a meeting at Ankie Spitzer's home with several families of those killed in Munich.

"It was a very important and special meeting where I met the kids and the widows, and I saw the look in their eyes of people who had sent their beloved ones to the Olympic Games and got them back dead," said Arad. "When I left the house, they gave me a small book, and they hugged me. I decided that, if I won an Olympic medal, I would dedicate this medal to the families and, of course, the victims."

The 1992 Summer Games in Barcelona were the first Olympics at which women's judo was a medal competition. Arad, who was twenty-five at the time, competed in the women's half-middleweight category. In the finals, she faced off against judoka Catherine Fleury of France in a close match, but ultimately lost when the judges' split decision left the referee breaking the tie in favor of Fleury.

"When I stood on the podium, crying from winning the first medal for Israel, but also from losing in the final, I looked at the Israeli flag and felt so proud," said Arad.

Following the match, Arad attended a press conference with some 150 journalists from all over the world.

"Today we close the circle in Israeli sport," she told the press. "After twenty years, we proved that Israeli sport didn't die with the victims in Munich. Today, I dedicate this medal to the families and the victims."

In her interview for our documentary, she said, "It was a very special moment. When you're on the top of the world, this is the time to give back to the community you come from."

Arad returned to Israel a national hero and remains a leader in Israeli sports.

CHAPTER 4

REMEMBERING THE ELEVEN

"We know we have to remember. We have to remember who we are; we have to remember where we came from. We also know that you have to forgive–forgive, but not forget."

–Michal Shahar, daughter of shooting coach Kehat Shorr

EVERY YEAR SINCE 1972, Israel has held memorial ceremonies on September 5 in schools, army units, sports centers, and other public arenas across the country. Before sports delegations leave Israel to compete in events—especially before the Olympics—the team holds a special ceremony to honor and remember the eleven lost Olympians. Central to these events are the loved ones who were left in the wake of the terrorist attack in Munich.

"Every event we do, they come. They see us and we see them as part of one big family created in September of 1972," said Igal Carmi, who was elected president of the Israel Olympic Committee in 2013. "They were very young—we have to remember that. They were kids or young wives, and we've grown up together since then—them as human beings and us as an organization with a very strong memory that this event shouldn't be forgotten."

When we interviewed Carmi for the *Munich '72 and Beyond* documentary, he shared how the murder of the eleven athletes is so crucial to the Israeli experience that the account of the attack has been incorporated into their education system.

"You ask any of the students, and they can name the names and tell you how they died. Streets, neighborhoods, stadiums carry their names. It is kept in the forefront of Israeli memory," he said. "In Israel we have many terror attacks that have killed many people in different ways. But this event caught everybody—to go to the Olympic Games, somewhere so peaceful, and not to come back, to have a big murder like that in Germany is something that won't be forgotten."

Those of us with the Foundation for Global Sports development have met many of the surviving family members over the years at different Olympiads. During the filming of *Munich '72 and Beyond*, our production team felt honored that these surviving relatives entrusted to us the stories of their beloved husbands and fathers. Though these men may be well known in Israel, we hope to ensure they are remembered throughout the world.

DAVID BERGER, 28, WEIGHTLIFTER
Born May 24, 1944, David Berger grew up in the Shaker Heights suburb of Cleveland, Ohio, one of three children to parents Dr. Benjamin and Dorothy Berger. He first started weightlifting at age thirteen. Astute in both academics and athletics, David later earned a bachelor's degree in psychology from Tulane University, where he also won an NCAA weightlifting championship in the 148-pound class. He went on to earn an MBA and a law degree from Columbia University in 1969. That same year, David won gold medals at the Maccabiah Games in Israel and the US Junior National Weightlifting championship in the middleweight class.

"He was funny, he was so smart," said his mother, Dorothy Berger, in an interview with ABC Sports in 2005. "He used to pick me up—he was so strong—and I'd holler, 'Put me down! Put me down!'"[15]

In 1970, rather than joining a prestigious New York City law firm, David immigrated to Israel, retaining dual US-Israeli citizenship, with the intent to open a law office in Tel Aviv upon completion of his military service with the Israel Defense Forces. While he trained to make the Israeli Olympic team, he coached disabled athletes.[16]

Yossef Romano, David Berger, and two other Israeli athletes train for the Olympics.
(Photo courtesy of the Berger family)

David went on to win a silver medal at the 1971 Asian Weightlifting Championships and secured a spot on the 1972 Israeli Olympic team. In Munich, David competed on September 2 as a light-heavyweight weightlifter, but was eliminated in an early round.

David's parents learned of the siege in Munich over breakfast, when Dr. Berger's secretary called and alerted him to turn on the television.

"We stayed glued to the television set until late that night," Dr. Berger told ABC Sports.

Jim McKay later wrote in his memoirs that, throughout his broadcast in Munich, he thought of David Berger, knowing he would be the person who told his parents whether their son had lived or died.

According to an autopsy report, David wasn't killed by gunfire—he received a nonfatal wound to his thigh—but died from smoke inhalation in the burning helicopter. US president Richard Nixon personally called David's parents to ask how he could help. Dr. Berger wanted to bring his son home for burial in the States, so a US Air Force strategic airlifter was dispatched to Munich to transport David's remains back to his family in Ohio.

The David Berger National Memorial, a sculpture commissioned by friends of his parents, was authorized by Congress and recognized by the US Department of the Interior as a national historic landmark. The sculpture, whose design features five Olympic rings broken in half, sits on the grounds of the Mandel Jewish Community Center near Cleveland.[17]

David's alma mater, Shaker Heights High School, where he competed in wrestling and golf, continues to honor his legacy. The school's fitness room is named after him, and every year the athletics department presents the David Berger Award to the top student-athlete of the senior class.[18]

ANTON FLIEGERBAUER, 32, GERMAN POLICE OFFICER

Born March 5, 1940, Anton Fliegerbauer

grew up with two siblings on their parents' farm in Westerndorf, Lower Bavaria. He initially attended agricultural school and then enrolled in training with the Bavarian State Police. He met his wife, Maria, in 1964 at a dance. They married in 1966; their son, Alfred, was born two years later.

During the Munich Games, Fliegerbauer was assigned to a mobile squad of the rapid reaction police unit. On September 5, his squad was ordered to Fürstenfeldbruck, where the police were trying to free the hostages.

A helicopter pilot was seriously injured during the gunfight that ensued that night. Fliegerbauer was fatally wounded shortly after the operation began.[19]

ZE'EV FRIEDMAN, 28, WEIGHTLIFTER

After his parents fled Poland to escape the Nazis, Ze'ev Friedman was born June 10, 1944, in Prokopyevsk, Siberia, in the former Soviet Union. His family moved back to Poland before immigrating to Israel in 1960, where Friedman started out his athletic career in gymnastics before switching to weightlifting. He served in the Israeli Air Force and fought in the 1967 Six-Day War. Friedman went on to become a physical education teacher and a champion weightlifter in the bantamweight division. He won seventh place in the 1969 World Weightlifting Championship in Warsaw, Poland, and he won third place in the 1971 Asian Weightlifting Championships in Manila, Philippines.[20] The following year at the Munich Olympics, Friedman finished in twelfth place, which was considered one of the best Olympic showings by an Israeli weightlifter up to that time.

Friedman died from gunshot wounds in one of the helicopters on the Fürstenfeldbruck airfield.

YOSSEF GUTFREUND, 40, WRESTLING REFEREE

Born on November 1, 1931, Yossef Gutfreund, along with his family, survived the

Holocaust in various hiding places in Romania and Hungary.[21]

Gutfreund attended medical school in Romania intending to become a veterinarian, but he found his work and passion in wrestling. He later immigrated to Israel in 1948 and went on to serve in the 1956 Sinai Campaign and the 1967 Six-Day War. He married his wife, Rachel, in 1956.

The 1972 Summer Games in Munich were Gutfreund's third Olympics. On the morning of September 5, as the terrorists forced their way inside the Israeli dorms, Gutfreund, which means "good friend," threw his massive weight against the door of the room he shared with weightlifting coach Tuvia Sokolsky. His heroic effort and shouts of warning allowed Sokolsky to escape through a back window.

Gutfreund and his wife had two daughters, Judith and Yael, who were fourteen and twelve at the time of the attack. In a 2002 interview with the *Los Angeles*

Times, the sisters recounted being pulled out of school the day of the siege after classmates came up to them declaring, "They killed your father." The girls returned home to their distraught mother and waited for word from Munich. Early in the morning on September 6, a knock at their front door brought word. "My mother said, 'That's it. You don't have a father anymore,'" Judith told the *Los Angeles Times*.[22]

Gutfreund's daughters remember their father as a loving, gentle man who relished his life and loved his wife deeply. After his death, Rachel could barely function, and their daughters were left to carry the burden between them.

"I was jealous of my friends that had fathers," Yael said. "I didn't want to go to their house and they had a father there. Why did they have a father and I don't have?"[23]

As of 2002, Gutfreund had nine grandchildren, who were born long after his death in one of the two helicopters at Fürstenfeldbruck.

ELIEZER HALFIN, 24, WRESTLER

Eliezer Halfin was born on June 18, 1948, in Riga, Latvia, in the former USSR, the only son of a man who had lost his previous family in the Holocaust. As a young freestyle wrestler, Halfin competed for eleven years in the Soviet Union and finished fourth in the national youth division. Halfin immigrated to Israel with his family in 1969, completed the Hebrew course required of immigrants at a kibbutz near the national Wingate Institute for Physical Education and Sports,[24] and joined the Israeli national wrestling team. Just months before his death, he secured his Israeli citizenship, fulfilled his compulsory military duty, and began work as a car mechanic.

In Munich, Halfin completed his first wrestling match on August 27.[25] He was shot to death on the Fürstenfeldbruck airfield on the night of September 5.

In February of 2011, Halfin's Olympic ID

card, which had been kept secretly by a German police officer since 1972, was found and returned to his sister. Germany and Israel held a special ceremony in Jerusalem to commemorate the return of what was considered a precious artifact.[26]

YOSSEF ROMANO, 32, WEIGHTLIFTER

Yossef Romano was one of eleven children born in Benghazi, former Italian Libya, on April 15, 1940. When he was six, his family immigrated to the region that would become Israel in order to escape anti-Semitic persecution. As an adult, Yossef worked as an interior decorator, and during his service with the Israel Defense Forces, he fought in the 1967 Six-Day War. Yossef's weightlifting talent was discovered by chance when, around age twenty, he lifted a friend into the air at the beach.[27] He went on to become an internationally competitive weightlifter and was Israel's middleweight champion for ten years.

When he left for Munich, Yossef and his wife, Ilana, had been together for eight years and had three young daughters:

Ilana and Yossef Romano on their wedding day

Oshrat, who was six years old, Rachel, who was four, and Schlomit, who was just five months old. After his death, Ilana was left to raise their girls alone.

"I lost a best friend, a partner, the best father. He was an amazing person who never yelled at his kids—always very sweet and loving and caring," said Ilana, who was twenty-six when her husband was killed. "Oshrat was supposed to start first grade, and she told me she was very nervous and afraid. So Yossef sent us a tape that arrived at the beginning of September. He told Oshrat and her sisters he loved them very much, and he promised them it was his last time that he'd go away, and he promised to come back."

When she received the news Yossef was dead, Ilana lay in bed in anguish.

"Oshrat, Rachel, and Schlomit came to me. I looked at them and said to myself, 'Should I get up? Should I show that I'm strong, or just let time take its course?'" she said. "They were afraid to cry next to me because they didn't want to offend me. I pulled them close to me, hugged them, and said, 'Something terrible happened. Dad was murdered in the Munich Olympics, and I promise that your father's memory will never be forgotten. The whole world will know who your father was, Yossef Romano.'"

Though she was a little girl then, Oshrat remembers the commotion that broke out when her family and neighbors heard of the siege in the Olympic Village.

Yossef Romano was a champion weightlifter.

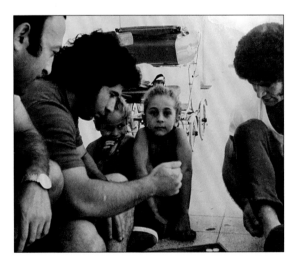

Weightlifting coach Tuvia Sokolsky and fellow athlete David Berger play backgammon with Yossef Romano and two of his young daughters.

Schlomit, Ilana, Oshrat, and Rachel Romano (Photos courtesy of the Romano family)

"Many people started coming to the house, and then when my father didn't call, we understood something was wrong," Oshrat recounted, during her interview for the documentary. "I remember people started shouting and crying, and then someone came and put me in my room. I was very proud that my father went to represent Israel. It was a very big a shock to understand that he came back in a coffin."

Oshrat paused, and when she looked up at our film crew again, her eyes were glistening.

"My father and mother were a simple family, a warm family," she continued. "We liked to go to the beach a lot, and I remember when someone got his car stuck in the sand, my father just took the car by his hands and pulled it out of the sand. It was to walk down the street and feel like you are with the king of the world. Children in our neighborhood would go after him and yell, 'Lift me, lift me!' I have many memories of him as a man that said whatever he thought, a very charismatic person."

Yossef Romano died trying to protect his teammates from their attackers. During competitions in Munich, he had injured his leg and was due to fly home on September 6 for an operation. He was hobbling on crutches up until the moment he threw them aside and charged the terrorists, wounding one of them before being shot.

"I'm not surprised that my father fought like that," said Oshrat. "That's who he was, that was his first intuition. He loved his friends very much and would do anything to defend them. It was probably very hard on their spirits to see him on the floor bleeding to death in that situation."

As an adult, Oshrat became a colonel in Israel's army. She was charged with serving families who lost children in the line of duty, a post that has brought meaning to her pain.

"At first I said no, I can't do this job. What happened to my father is with me all day, every day, for so many years—it's not something that's healed. I thought, I can't help other people," she said. "My boss said, 'Listen, we need you—you can do it.' I didn't believe it, but I came to the houses and helped these families who lost their boys or father. I realized it's something that lifts you up—to know the pain, to live it—to know how to help other people who've just lost their dearest family members. I am the person I am now because of what has happened to us."

Though Yossef is gone, Ilana still senses his spirit: "He's present every place. He's there all the time, for sure. If not, I wouldn't have the force to fight for so much time."

"My dad would be proud of my mother, how she raised three daughters alone," Oshrat told us. "She had to think about feeding us, how to give us confidence and understanding that life goes on, and yet to not forget."

Her voice broke, and she paused to wipe tears from her face.

"If he were alive today, he wouldn't believe what my mother has done in fighting for a memorial," she continued, "because it's very difficult to act like life goes on, but to keep fighting, to not give up. I don't think he knew what kind of woman he married. Life taught my mother to be strong, and I admire her. She is a very impressive woman."

AMITZUR SHAPIRA, 40,
TRACK AND FIELD COACH

Amitzur Shapira was born on July 9, 1932, in Tel Aviv, shortly after his parents emigrated from the Soviet Union. As a young man, Shapira excelled in track and field, especially as a sprinter and long jumper. He studied psychology, education, and literature in Tel Aviv and then sports at the Wingate sports center, where he taught for many years after retiring from competitions. Shapira coached the national track and field team, which he accompanied to the 1964 Olympic Games in Tokyo, Japan.[28]

Considered the top track coach in Israel, Shapira discovered runner Esther Shahamorov Roth when she was only fourteen, and coached her toward Olympic- level competition for the next six years.

Shahamorov was favored to win Israel's first medal in the 1972 Munich Summer Games. On September 4, 1972, she qualified for the 100-meter hurdles semifinals,

Esther Roth Shahamorov, Shapira's star track and field athlete

setting an Israeli record. Shapira, who was like a father to her, was waiting for her at the finish line, his face beaming with joy.[29]

The semifinals were to take place the next day, but Shapira, who had a wife and four children back in Israel, died in one of the helicopters at Fürstenfeldbruck. Shahamorov returned to Israel with her surviving teammates.

KEHAT SHORR, 53, SHOOTING COACH

 Born on February 21, 1919, Kehat Shorr the senior member of the 1972 Israeli Olympic delegation. Shorr was a decorated marksman who had resisted the Nazis in his native Romania during the Second World War. He was part of a group hiding in the Carpathian Mountains that snuck into Romanian cities to rescue other Jews from the Holocaust. He married his wife, Sarah, in 1946, and his daughter, Michal, was born three years later.[30] On September 5, 1963, Shorr and

his family finally immigrated to Israel after years of vain attempts.

His reputation as a shooting coach back in Romania preceded him. Upon arrival in Tel Aviv, he was immediately asked to coach the Israeli national shooting team, and he later accompanied them to the 1968 Olympic Games in Mexico City.

"When we lived in Romania, in the winter it was impossible to go shooting outside," said his daughter, Michal Shahar. "So all his shooting students came to our home to train. I heard him always say, 'You must be the best. You must do the best.' His best legacy is that I meet a lot of people who know who my father was, and they say, 'I got this job, I'm in this post, because of your father.'"

In Munich, Shorr supervised the two marksmen who had qualified for the Games, Henry Hershkovitz and Zelig Shtorch, who both managed to escape 31 Connollystrasse when the others were taken hostage.[31]

Michal was a young newlywed when her father was killed at Fürstenfeldbruck.

"I was at home in the morning. I open, like always, the news, and they're talking about the eleven athletes in Munich. At this point, I didn't know that my father was one of them, because my mother was in Romania," said Michal. "My mother came home, and we were waiting all day for news, hoping all the time that it was a mistake. By evening I understood that he was one of them, and they even showed for a moment a picture of him. Late that day, they told us everything is okay, and then—you know the end."

Along with Ankie Spitzer and Ilana Romano, Michal has been one of the family members fighting for a moment of silence to remember her late father and the other athletes.

"For me, I am living this moment every day," said Michal. "My home, where I live, is not far. It's two minutes from the grave of my father. I think of him every week. My son has my father's name. I speak his name every day. My daughter decided when she got married to take my family's name, Shorr. My mother, who is ninety, is still living, and she also speaks every day of him."

Shorr's legacy is also carried on through his children, grandchildren, and great-grandchildren.

"I have a grandchild who is eight years old. He lives now in California, because my son works there. My son once called me and said, 'Your grandson wants to speak with you.' At school, they have to read a biography. My grandson decided to read the biography of my father, whom he never knew of course. I asked how he thought of that idea. My son said, 'You know, because my name is Kehat, the Israelis I meet in the States ask me if my name is Kehat because of Kehat Shorr. I say yes, my grandfather is Kehat Shorr.' So this is how my grandson decided to do the biography of my father."

As an adult, Michal earned a degree in mathematics and became a high school teacher, eventually becoming a school principal. Both in her family and at her school, she ensures that the memory of her father and the attack on his team are never forgotten.

"I think it's very important that the new generations remember this story," she said. "That's why at my school, the teams have a Sports Day every year as a day of remembrance for the eleven. They invite the families, and they give first place in the competitions in the name of the eleven. We know we have to remember. We have to remember who we are; we have to remember where we came from. We also know that you have to forgive—forgive, but not forget. This is what I teach my children."

MARK SLAVIN, 18, WRESTLER

Mark Slavin was the youngest of the eleven Israeli athletes. Born on January 31, 1954, the eldest of his parents' four children, Mark grew up in Minsk, Belarus, where he was taunted mercilessly for being Jewish. He took an interest in street fighting and asked his maternal grandfather to help him learn to fight.

Mark Slavin

His grandfather, a former weightlifter, introduced him to the wrestling ring. Mark fell in love with the sport and rose to the top ranks in his country. In 1971, he won the Soviet middleweight junior wrestling championship, and in 1972, he won a spot on the Russian Olympic team. But his heart called him elsewhere.

"He told my parents that he wanted to represent the Jewish people, and not the Russian people," said Mika Slavin, who was born two years after her brother's death. "Many Jews left Russia in this era, and Mark checked everything out without even telling my parents. Then he said, 'Listen, I'm going to Israel. I want to represent Israel in the Olympics.'"

Mark's father protested, pointing out that the Munich Games were just months away.

"Mark said, 'If you don't want to come with me, I'm going by myself,'" recounted Mika. "Then my mom said, 'No way.' All of my family—twenty-five people—made aliyah in May of 1972 because of my brother. They all moved to Israel not knowing anything."

Mark arrived at the Israeli wrestling club with none of his medals or trophies or other proof of his talents. Moshe Weinberg, the wrestling coach for the Israeli Olympic team, tested Mark's strength and abilities against twenty-four-year-old Eliezer Halfin. (Both Weinberg and Halfin later perished alongside the young Russian.) Mark won match after match against experienced wrestlers—including French Olympic medalist Daniel Robin—and secured his spot on the Israeli Olympic team.

"However, there was a rule in the government that you cannot represent Israel if you don't live there for three years," said Mika, "The Knesset [Israeli parliament] changed the law so my brother could go to the Olympics. He was very excited because it was his dream to join the Israeli team and to represent the Jewish people. He said to my dad, 'Even if nothing will happen, I was there.' That was his dream."

Considered a strong medal contender, Mark died at Fürstenfeldbruck before his dream could be fully realized. His first match was to be the same day the terrorists invaded 31 Connollystrasse.

The Slavin family shortly before Mark's death

Mark Slavin wrestling with a friend, 1968 (Photos courtesy of the Slavin family)

Though Mika, who bears a striking resemblance to her oldest brother, never knew Mark, his presence has pervaded her life from the start.

"I was born into that tragedy," she said. "My parents weren't young—my mom was forty-two—and they each got sick after I was born. I remember my mom crying a lot. I would sit on her lap all my childhood and just sweep the tears off her face. They were great parents, but it was very sad. My brother was there all the time."

Married and the mother of two daughters, Mika has become her family's spokesperson, and she's the keeper of Mark's training clothes, his goggles, and his fighting gloves.

"My father used to be the representative of the family regarding my brother," she said. "He used to give interviews and lectures. When he died, I stepped into his shoes. My sister and brother aren't talking about it, so it's up to me to keep on telling the story."

ANDRE SPITZER, 27, FENCING COACH

The son of Holocaust survivors, Andre Spitzer was born in Romania on July 4, 1945. Andre and his mother moved to Israel in 1964, eight years after the death of his father. In Israel, Andre served in the Air Force and studied fencing at the National Sports Academy. Andre had been an enthusiastic fencer since his adolescence. In 1968, he enrolled in a two-year program to become a fencing master at the National Fencing Academy in the Netherlands, where he met Ankie, a Dutch national. The pair fell in love and married, and at the end of his term, Andre and Ankie returned to Israel.

"I was a fencer myself," explained Ankie, who was twenty-five when she married Andre. "My husband was my fencing coach. If I hadn't been pregnant, I would have also participated in the Olympics as one of his students. But I wanted to see what the whole dream was about, so I joined him."

The couple's daughter, Anouk, was born on June 27, 1972. Two months later, Andre and Ankie left their baby daughter in the care of Ankie's parents in Holland, and then traveled to Munich. Andre was at the Olympics to coach fencers Yehuda Weinstein and Dan Alon, two athletes who escaped the terrorist attack.

"I couldn't stay with him in the Olympic Village because back then it was divided into men's and women's dorms," said Ankie. "As we were only a young married couple, we decided to rent a small room in Munich so we could be together. I spent all day in the Olympic Village—it was easy to get in without credentials—or at the competitions. I could see the glory of the Olympics. I could feel it. It was wonderful."

After Andre finished his competitions, the young couple took a two-day excursion to Holland to visit their daughter, who had fallen sick and was in the hospital. Ankie decided to stay in Holland to be close to Anouk, but Andre was required to return to his team in Munich.

Andre and Ankie Spitzer on their wedding day

Ankie with baby daughter Anouk
(Photos courtesy of Ankie Spitzer)

"He didn't want to go," Ankie said. "I told him, 'You have to go back because you only got two days off from your team.' He said, 'Yeah, but I'd love to stay a few days with you and the baby.' But I knew he had to get back."

Ankie drove him to the train station for the twelve-hour ride back to Munich, but on they way Andre insisted on stopping by the hospital to kiss his little girl good-bye. By the time they reached the station, the train had departed. There wouldn't be another train until evening.

"I said, 'Let's try to pick up the train in the next station,' which was about thirty miles away," recounted Ankie. "I was driving like a madwoman because I didn't want him to get into trouble. I wanted him to reach that train."

At the next station, Ankie threw the car in park, and helped her husband jump onto the moving train as it was pulling out of the station.

"He didn't even have a ticket," she said.

"I started running along the train, and Andre said, 'Ankie, I'm going to call you tonight when I get back to Munich,' and he left. And I said, 'Thank God, at least he got on the train, and he'll get there tonight. He won't get into trouble.'"

That night Andre called Ankie, as he had promised.

"He told me, 'Ankie, I'm going to look for my room in the Israeli quarters,' because he'd never slept there. We had been sleeping in the little pension we'd found in the city. We talked a bit more, but he was on a pay phone and had only a half a mark left. He said, 'I'll call you tomorrow to let you know when we're leaving, so you'll know when to take the plane back to Israel.' Then he had only a few pennies left, and he said, 'I love you, love you!' And that was it."

The photo of Andre Spitzer standing in the window at the mercy of the terrorists has since become one of the most iconic images of the terrorist attack.

Since Munich, Ankie has had a long career

as a correspondent for Dutch and Belgian television, covering politics in the Middle East.

"I get to go around to many of the Arab countries, definitely in the Palestinian territories. Before I started to do this work, I had to decide, 'Am I able to do this? Am I able to talk to the people in Gaza or the West Bank without extra thoughts after what happened to my husband?' I decided I was able to do it, or else I wouldn't have taken the job. I've been doing this work for the past twenty-five years. It's a very lively region in the Middle East, and I've seen all the different aspects of the conflict. I feel blessed to do this work."

Ankie remarried, but later divorced. She has raised four children—"my big joy," she said—and has two grandchildren.

"What we're doing with the memory of the victims—it's not my hobby nor my obsession," she said. "I have a full life. Munich is part of my life, and it will never go away, but I'm very privileged and thankful that I have this life with my children and my work."

YAKOV SPRINGER, 51, WEIGHTLIFTING JUDGE

Yakov Springer was born in Kalisz, Poland, on June 10, 1921. He was the only member of his large family to survive the Holocaust. His parents and siblings were deported to the Litzmannstadt Ghetto and subsequently murdered, while Yakov escaped to the Soviet Union. After the war, he returned alone to Poland where he married his wife, Shoshana, in 1951 and had two children.[32] Yakov immersed himself into sports and physical education and went on to represent Poland in the 1956 Summer Olympics in Melbourne, Australia.

"My father was an excellent sportsman and a coach, and he had a very important place in the sports community in Poland," said his son, Alex. "In 1967, after he was married and had me and my sister—I was twelve and she was five—he decided to come to Israel. He felt in Israel his life would be much more safe and secure. My father was also my teacher—he taught physical education at the school where I studied. Here, he started to build athletics, and he became a coach of the Israeli team for the Olympic Games. He believed in sport as a way of life. To be good in sport could gain results in other fields of life. This is what he taught me."

The 1972 Summer Games in Munich were Yakov's fifth Olympics.

"He was a referee, an international judge," said Alex. "It was very important to him to come back to Germany because Germany was responsible for the murder of all his family. He came as a sportsman: 'You weren't successful in destroying all my family—I am here. My sports team is here with me, so you didn't win.' It was important to him to close this circle. We were very proud about it."

The day his father was killed, sixteen-year-old Alex was at school. Around noon, he returned home where his mother and sister were waiting. All day they listened to the radio, waiting for word on the safety of the athletes.

"After they said on the radio that the sportsmen had been freed, and everything was okay, all the neighbors came to our house with Champagne and congratulations," remembered Alex. "We were very happy, and we went to sleep with the idea that everything was okay. By five or six o'clock in the morning, somebody from the Israeli Olympic community knocked on our door and told us it wasn't true. All were killed, including my father. And that's it. It was very surprising and very shocking."

Because Yakov was an international judge, he had been assigned quarters separate from the Israeli delegation.

"He was supposed to sleep in a different place—not those apartments with the Israeli team," said Alex. "But because he loved his students so much, he decided to stay with them, and that was the biggest tragedy, because he wasn't supposed to be there."

Alex Springer is now a family physician and psychotherapist who works in Holon, a city near Tel Aviv. He described his father as very ambitious, a perfectionist, someone who believed that success was attainable through training and hard work. He also described someone of generous spirit: Yakov opened a community center to mentor young people from poor, rough, crime-ridden neighborhoods. He instilled in them a work ethic and used sports to improve their academic performance in school.

"At his funeral, all these children came," said Alex, "and it was really hard for them to say goodbye because he was like their spiritual father. Every year when they have a memorial ceremony in Holon, a small team from the school where he taught comes with their teacher, and they tell them about what kind of person he was, and about what happened. What's important is to keep telling the story." Alex is himself a father—"three boys," he told us, as a huge smile lit up his face. He endeavors to pass onto his sons the values his father instilled in him.

"I teach them also not to hate, because it won't bring us anywhere toward peace and love. It won't fix what happened. That's the most important thing I want them to know," he said.

MOSHE WEINBERG, 32, WRESTLING COACH

 Moshe Weinberg was born in Haifa, Israel, on September 19, 1939, after his family fled the Nazis in Vienna in 1938. After his parents separated, Weinberg was raised by his grandmother. His neighbor Erwin Becker, a former wrestler from Germany, introduced Weinberg to the sport and began coaching him.[33]

Weinberg won the national youth wrestling championship and went on to be Israel's middleweight wrestling champion for eight years. Weinberg coached at the Wingate Institute, the national physical education and sports center in Netanya, and was the wrestling coach for the 1972 Israeli Olympic team.

He had been married for only eleven months when he left for Munich, leaving his wife with their newborn son, Guri, who was a month old at the time. In his heroic attempts to protect his teammates, Weinberg became the first casualty of the terrorist attack.

THEIR LEGACY LIVES ON

After the eleven Olympians were laid to rest, their surviving loved ones poured their grief and rage into the fight for justice and recognition. But many of them waged another kind of battle as well—one in which their souls might attain some measure of peace beyond the pain.

"For two months I walked around full of anger and hatred," said Ankie. "I didn't know what to do. I was in Israel, but I didn't speak the language. I had a two-month-old baby. I didn't know a soul here, and all my family was back in Holland. After two months so full of hatred, I said to myself, 'How am I going to raise my daughter with hate in my heart? She cannot come to understand what happened if I'm full of hate.' So I worked on myself

to make a change, and what all the families tried to do was to educate and raise our children without hate in our hearts."

One of Ankie's happiest moments after losing her husband happened at the 1996 Summer Olympics in Atlanta, Georgia.

"Ilana and I took all the children—the fourteen orphans whose fathers were killed," she said. "Many of those children never knew their fathers. These kids have always lived in the shadow of the Olympics. The Olympics were always something negative. What we wanted to do was to show them what the Games are really like, the glory of the Olympics, the wonderful feeling of being at the Opening Ceremony and seeing all these delegations walk in and feel part of it. So we did."

Oshrat Romano, Ilana and Yossef's eldest daughter, was moved by the sight of her people in the Parade of Nations.

"I remember the Israeli delegation was in the stadium and going with the flags

The Opening Ceremony of the 1996 Atlanta Games (David Taylor/Getty Images)

and it was like seeing my father and his friends," she said.

When Ankie arrived in Atlanta, she learned that, for the first time in Olympic history, a Palestinian delegation would be participating in the Games.

"The Olympic movement wants everyone on the planet to feel as if they have a chance to compete under their flag," explained sportswriter Jeremy Schaap.

"The IOC is not qualified to determine what is a country or what isn't a country, but historically it's had entities compete that aren't countries—overseas territories, dominions, possessions. It would seem in many respects that Palestine and Palestinians qualified under the Olympic auspices to present a team."

Ankie broached the subject with the Israeli children, most of whom were teenagers by that time.

"I said, 'You should know that the Palestinians have a delegation. What are you going to do when they walk in?' They didn't really understand my question. They said, 'They're athletes, right? We're going to applaud them, too.' And I said, 'Yes, but there's no connotation with the Palestinians?' 'No,' they said, 'these people were not the murderers who killed our fathers. They aren't responsible for what happened then.'

"That was the moment I said to myself, 'Ah, maybe our wish to educate them without hate in their heart, that is what came out here.' That is what I see in these kids. This was the point I wanted to reach. And I watched them when the Palestinian delegation came in—only very few people—and they stood up and applauded them."

While the Israeli families were in Atlanta, the local Jewish community and the Israeli consulate hosted a Sabbath memorial service for the eleven athletes who had died in Munich.

"I took my sixteen-year-old daughter to this special dinner event," said Steven Ungerleider, author and producer on the *Munich '72 and Beyond* documentary. "Among the many diplomats and dignitaries was the then mayor of Jerusalem, Ehud Barak, who later became prime minister of Israel. Of all of the memorial services for the Israeli athletes that I have attended over the years, this one was truly special."

"I met the head of the Palestinian delegation," said Ankie, "and I asked him if he would like to come and meet the children of the athletes from Munich. And he said, 'I would be honored.' He and three other Palestinian officials attended the memorial. I introduced them to all the children, and they embraced and kissed."

During the reception, Oshrat gave a speech to the attendees and guests.

"Afterward, the head of the Palestinian delegation came and hugged me and kissed me on the forehead," said Oshrat. "I felt that though cruel people did what they did, maybe other people can fix it by understanding it was such a very bad thing, so they won't do something so traumatic to anyone else."

"For me, that was the most significant thing in connection to the children—that they aren't walking around with hatred," noted Ankie. "Of course they don't love—far from it—the people who killed their fathers. That's a different thing. But that doesn't mean you have to hate a whole people because of the sins of a few. This is what is apparent now, and I'm very happy about it. We don't hate."

The IOC recognized the Palestinian delegation for the first time at the 1996 Atlanta Games. (Romeo Gacad/AFP/Getty Images)

PART 3

THE MUNICH MEMORIAL

CHAPTER 5

A CHAMPION EMERGES

"Munich needed time to work through the shock to its consciousness. I myself could only go back to Connollystrasse for the first time ten years later."

—Ludwig Spaenle, minister of education and culture, Bavaria, Germany

OVER THE ENSUING DECADES, the widows of the eleven raised their children, who then married and had children of their own. Each new generation joined the previous generation in seeking and waiting for recognition of their loved ones. During filming for the *Munich'72 and Beyond* documentary, we interviewed Bavarian minister Ludwig Spaenle, who was only eleven when the massacre happened. He described to us his hometown's slow progression toward reckoning with the disaster.

"This attack intended to destroy this unique sports festival was a shock that the city and I have never forgotten," he said. "Munich needed time to work through this shock to its consciousness. I myself could only go back to Connollystrasse for the first time ten years later."

The buildings in the Olympic Village that once hosted international athletes now house local Munich residents. On our visits to Munich over the years, we have always been puzzled as to why there wasn't much there to remember such a significant historical event.

Outside the bright blue door at 31 Connollystrasse stands a stone memorial plaque on which the names of the dead are engraved in German and Hebrew. Visitors who have made a pilgrimage to this place have left piles of rocks on top

The Fritz Koenig memorial stands in tribute to the murdered Israeli athletes and the fallen German police officer. *(Stuart Forster Europe / Alamy Stock Photo)*

of the plaque as a sign of respect for the victims. For some of the victims' survivors, however, this monument feels like an afterthought.

"I went to Munich a few years ago and was very disappointed," said Mika Slavin, sister of slain athlete Mark Slavin. "There was nothing—a little memorial on Connolly Street that you have to look for. It was unbelievable that people live in this apartment, and they don't even know what happened there."

In the years since the massacre, other markers of remembrance have emerged. On the trail from the Olympic Village to the Olympic Stadium sits a memorial sculpture by Bavarian sculptor Fritz Koenig. The sculpture, which was dedicated in October of 1995, is a long, rectangular beam of granite with the Israeli athletes' names inscribed in Hebrew and the West German police officer's name in Latin. At its base, a metal plaque reads, "A boundary stone of life, but not of the idea—During the Games of the Twentieth Olympiad in Munich, eleven Israeli athletes and one German police officer suffered a violent death in a terrorist attack on September 5, 1972."

We were not alone in noticing that the existing monuments to the Munich massacre seemed disproportionately small compared to the magnitude of the tragedy.

"There is a very small memorial outside the Olympic Stadium, but for me personally it's spooky small," noted Frank Shorter, who won gold in the men's marathon after the massacre in 1972. "It sits in the same place where forty years ago I made the decision not to let the terrorist attack affect me."

Around the fortieth anniversary of the Munich massacre, however, the contemporary generation of German leaders began discussing ways to create a more dignified memorial that would tell the full story and place the events in a historical context.

THE LAUNCH OF THE MUNICH 1972 MASSACRE MEMORIAL

On September 5, 2012, Bavarian officials hosted a fortieth anniversary commemoration at the Fürstenfeldbruck airport where nine of the eleven Israeli hostages were killed. More than five hundred people attended the service. Among the group were IOC president Jacques Rogge, IOC vice president Thomas Bach, Israeli deputy prime minister Silvan Shalom, and German officials including Bavarian prime minister Horst Seehofer and minister of the interior Hans-Peter Friedrich. At the start of the ceremony, German, Bavarian, and Israeli flags were lowered to half-mast, and mourners lit candles in remembrance of the men who died on those grounds.

An Israeli delegation that included family members of the victims, athletes who survived the terrorist attack, and

Surviving family members light candles to remember their lost loved ones at the fortieth anniversary event held at Fürstenfeldbruck airfield in Munich. (Thomas Niedermueller/Getty Images)

Ankie Spitzer delivers a speech during the commemoration of the fortieth anniversary of the terrorist attack in Munich. (Guenter Schiffmann/AFP/Getty Images)

Olympic committee officials had been flown to Germany, courtesy of Lufthansa. Munich's collective pain over what had happened to the Israeli athletes in their backyard did not go unnoticed by the Israelis in attendance.

"I was in Munich for the commemoration of forty years," said Michal Shahar, daughter of shooting coach Kehat Shorr. "We met at the press conference some of the ministers there, and we sensed they were really sorry and that they were trying to do their best now."

The Bavarian ministers began discussing a way to more formally memorialize the tragedy near the Olympic Village where the terrorist attack occurred. Their idea to build a larger, more official memorial started to take shape.

"The remembrance convention at Fürstenfeldbruck airport spawned the idea—perhaps a little late, but it was the right time to be able to create a new place and a new way of remembrance," explained Spaenle.

"Having something that memorializes what happened in the Olympic Village is the most important thing to show what happened there more than forty years ago," noted Ankie Spitzer.

"I am a true believer that when the time is right, things will happen," said Shorter, regarding the creation of a memorial at long last. "As we age, we get to certain points where memories are important, and we arrived at that point where many of the people who experienced this tragedy in Munich were starting to pass on. There was an awakening, saying, 'Many of us now are going to be gone, and it's important that this not be forgotten.'"

In September of 2012, Bavarian prime minister Seehofer made a state visit to Israel where he announced his plans to build a memorial in Munich. A year later, on Wednesday, September 4, 2013, the Bavarian Ministry of Education and Cultural Affairs held a press conference to formally announce the creation of the Munich Massacre Memorial. Diplomats from Chancellor Angela Merkel's office, the Bavarian ministry, the consul general of Israel, the victims' relatives, the director of the Jewish Museum in Munich, and architects with expertise in cultural sites of remembrance were slated to convene in order to establish the guidelines for the memorial as a place to mourn and remember.

"With the new memorial, we have a place where the historical situation will be explained in a new, modern way, a very surprising way," said Spaenle. "The discussions about this memorial were important for our city. We have contacts around the world with the IOC, the German Olympic Sports Association, and the Israel government. I was able to talk about the plans of the memorial in Jerusalem and received a very positive reaction."

"We think this new generation of people—like Dr. Spaenle, the Bavarian minister, and Dr. Seehofer, the prime minister of Bavaria—all these people have a totally different outlook," said Ankie. "They understand the importance. They are open-minded, and they helped us enormously. The memorial is absolutely what we wanted for such a long time. We are more than happy and grateful about this memorial."

"It took forty years to deal with the memory of the massacre," said Bernhard Purin, the director of the Jewish Museum in Munich and a member of the Munich Memorial project team. "In my opinion, the reason was that the attack didn't fit the new image of Munich in Bavaria—an open, bright city. No one wanted to deal with it, and it's taken this long to realize we need to commemorate it. The generations responsible are gone, and the newer generations have an easier time dealing with this disaster."

The families of the eleven have found healing in the genuine concern and compassion demonstrated by their contemporaries in Germany.

"It's really moving to know someone cares," said Oshrat Romano Kandell. "It's not only words. They're doing something for the history—that people will know and ask what happened. It's not hiding, even when not everything was good. The heart and the intention behind the memorial, it's very touching."

Just as a new, more forward-thinking generation of leaders had emerged in Germany, elections at the IOC—which now managed the Olympic participation of more than two hundred countries—were ushering in a new president who would finally answer the survivors' pleas for official recognition of the eleven Israeli Olympians. The man who would lead this paradigm shift at the IOC—a German and a former Olympian himself—was Dr. Thomas Bach.

THE RISE OF DR. THOMAS BACH

Born in West Germany in 1953, Thomas Bach studied law and politics at the University of Würzburg, and after completing his doctorate in law, founded his own law firm. Dr. Bach joined the IOC in 1991, and over the next two decades served the organization in a number of critical capacities, including chairing key committees and twice holding the vice presidency. He was elected the ninth president in IOC history on September 10, 2013.

As an athlete, Dr. Bach was a champion fencer: in team foil fencing, he won World Championships in 1976 and 1977, and he won gold with the West German men's team at the 1976 Montreal Summer Games. Dr. Bach is the third IOC president to have been an Olympian, and the only one with an Olympic gold medal.

"Thomas Bach is a man for the times," said Barry Maister, former New Zealand field hockey player and IOC member. "He is a very open, transparent reformer. He's an insightful and intelligent person. He reflects and gives considered views, but above all of those qualities, he's a sportsman. He understands what it means to represent your country. He understands what it means to stand on the victory dais. That is huge. You can't buy that. You can't replicate that. If you've

Thomas Bach (center) and his fencing team celebrate winning a gold medal at the 1976 Olympic Games in Montreal, Canada. *(Müller X/ullstein bild/Getty Images)*

stood on an Olympic dais, you've got something that people can't even imagine. That identifies you."

As a young Olympian, Dr. Bach knew several of the Israeli athletes who died in Munich, and over the decades with the IOC, he came to know their family members as well.

"I had a special relationship with Thomas Bach because I knew him from fencing competitions, long before he became vice president or president of the IOC," said Ankie. "I believe in Thomas Bach. First of all, he's a fencer, and fencers are a special breed. They're not the same as other athletes. The word of honor—when they greet, they have respect for their opponent, and they accept the judgment of the judge. And even if you lose, you salute your opponent. From a fencer, I

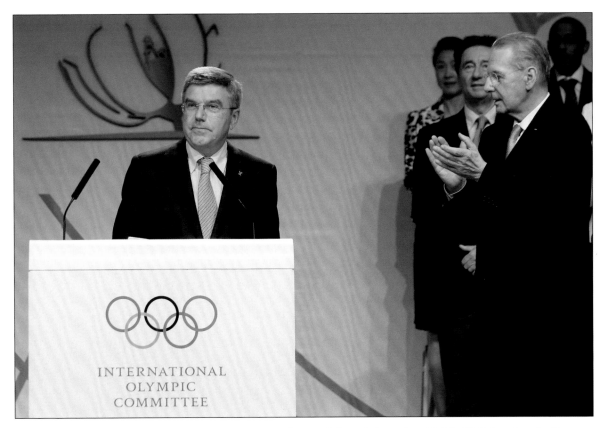

Dr. Thomas Bach was elected the ninth president of the IOC at the 125th IOC Session in Buenos Aires, Argentina. *(Ian Walton/Getty Images)*

expect more than from anybody else."

The families of the eleven, Ankie said, were happy when Bach was nominated to be president.

"We sent him a letter, and said as families we very much hope he will be elected because we know he has his heart in the right place," she said. "He remembers what happened in Munich, but he's from a different generation. And when he was elected, we wrote him to congratulate him. I expected from him to do the right thing."

Those of us with the Foundation for Global Sports Development have attended fourteen Olympiads to date, and it appeared that previous IOC presidents and past boards feared that doing something for the Israelis would incur the wrath of their

Saudi delegates and other Arab constituencies. The election of Dr. Thomas Bach was a turning point in this process. It had troubled Dr. Bach for years that nothing had been done to commemorate the eleven Israeli Olympians, and he was the first one who was willing to take any political heat that might befall him.

"Things are different under Thomas Bach," noted Jeremy Schaap. "He's German, he lived through Munich, and he has competed in the Olympics himself. He has an appreciation his immediate predecessors didn't have for the magnitude of the tragedy in Munich."

Once he had assumed the IOC presidency, Dr. Bach pledged the IOC's full support—including a financial contribution of $250,000—to the creation of the Munich 1972 Massacre Memorial, and he announced plans to officially recognize the Israeli athletes at the 2016 Rio Summer Olympics.

As we have heard Dr. Bach eloquently say, "We are a family, and we must support this memorial as a family. We must make sure that we look after each other, and make sure there is honor brought to the family and to the victims."

"I think Thomas Bach is doing here a great move, said Igal Carmi, who was elected president of the Israel Olympic Committee in 2013. "He was very supportive of us from day one. In his own way, he's moving the entire movement toward the right recognition, and I trust him very much that he's going to do it the best."

"Over the years, I have met with Dr. Bach and members of his staff to ensure a solid dialog on all logistics pertaining to the memorial," said Steven Ungerleider, author and producer of *Munich '72 and Beyond*. "President Bach is a breath of fresh air—not only with his initiative to preserve the memory of Munich, but in other areas of sport. Of the last five IOC presidents I have known, he is the first who really cares about the integrity of the athletes and who advocates for them.

Israel sent their largest ever delegation to Rio de Janeiro, Brazil, for the 2016 Summer Olympics.
(Clive Brunskill/Getty Images)

We are blessed to have him at the helm."

The German federal government and the Bavarian state government sponsored the memorial's construction, along with financial pledges from the IOC and our nonprofit, the Foundation for Global Sports Development.

"Memorials are important; remembrance

is important," said Schaap. "We have to constantly remind ourselves that these things happened, and they could happen again. And the Germany of today is, in many ways, doing a better job of confronting its past, whether the enormity of the Holocaust or the smaller-scale but nevertheless tragic events in Munich. They're doing an admirable job."

A MOMENT OF SILENCE, AT LAST

For more than forty years, the Israeli widows and their children asked the IOC for official recognition of their loved ones, and they endured bitter disappointment at each of the ensuing Summer Olympics—ten in all—since Munich. But with Dr. Bach now leading the charge, their hope was renewed.

"After all these years of knocking on everybody's door—it was very tiring, very disappointing, and it assumed a lot of time, money, energy, mental focus—I'm still optimistic it will happen," said Ankie, during the filming of our documentary in 2014. "We won't rest until, at the Opening Ceremony or in the framework of the

Olympic Games, they mention what happened there. If we are already too old—Ilana, me, the other widows—our children will continue the fight, or the children of our children. I hope it's going to happen soon as my time is running out and also my energy, but we won't rest until we hear it, and we believe Thomas Bach will do it."

In the summer of 2016, Israel sent their largest Olympic delegation to Rio de Janeiro—forty-seven athletes competed in seventeen sports. While in Rio, the families of the eleven would witness a historic step by the IOC: at two official ceremonies, IOC president Thomas Bach planned to acknowledge the tragic loss of the eleven Olympians at the 1972 Munich Games.

"When we heard about it, it was a feeling of, 'Finally! Finally something happens,'" said Shahar. "I was sad that we had to wait so many years for something like this."

"I was a child when my father was killed," said Oshrat. "I'm now a mother. I grew up,

The Place of Mourning at the Rio Olympics featured two memorial stones.
(Edgard Garrido-Pool/Getty Images)

and I couldn't believe it was gonna happen. It's very moving that a German person decided to do it. For me, it's healing."

On Wednesday, August 3, 2016, two days ahead of the Opening Ceremony, the IOC held a memorial service in the Place of Mourning, a memorial site set up in a quiet, grassy outdoor area in Rio's Olympic Village, to honor fifteen people who died in the course of the Olympic Games. Among those honored were the eleven Israelis, the West German police officer, the two victims of the Centennial Park bombing at the 1996 Atlanta Summer Games, and Georgian luger Nodar Kumaritashvili, who died during a training run before the 2010 Vancouver Winter Games.

The Place of Mourning was to become a mainstay at future Olympics so athletes and guests could have a dignified place to remember family and friends who had passed away. In Rio, the area included a tree on whose branches were tied ribbons in Olympic colors, as well as a special memorial that featured a small stone perched on a larger stone—both from Ancient Olympia in Greece—housed in glass, with an inscription that said, "We will always remember you forever in our hearts."

Dr. Bach addressed the intimate gathering, which included other IOC officials, Ankie Spitzer, Ilana Romano, and members of the 2016 Israeli Olympic delegation: "We chose the Olympic Village as the location for the Place of Mourning because it symbolizes the unity of the Olympic family," he said.

Dr. Bach became emotional as he read the names of each of the eleven Israeli athletes.

"We commemorate them because this was an attack not only on our fellow Olympians, but also an assault on the values that the Olympic Village stands for," he told the mourners. "It was an attack on the universal power of sport to unite all of humanity in peace and solidarity. The Olympic Games are always an affirmation of life, so let our commemoration today also be an affirmation of their lives. Through this act of remembrance, the spirit of those who have departed continues to live on."

And, in answer to four decades of pleas, Dr. Bach led the group in observing a minute of silence.

After the service concluded, Dr. Bach leaned in to hug Ankie and Ilana, who were visibly moved. Though the recognition wasn't during the Opening Ceremony, the two widows found deep solace in this moment in Rio's Olympic Village.

"Everyone stood for a minute's silence inside the Village. It was everything we always wanted—it finally felt like closure," Ankie told the press after the event.

"This is an extremely emotional moment for us, one we have been waiting for since 1972. Our patience finally paid off. The memory of the eleven Munich victims has finally been acknowledged by the IOC," Ilana told reporters.

Ankie and Ilana were gifted with another moment of silence on Sunday, August 14, 2016, during a dedicated ceremony to honor the memory of the eleven Israeli Olympians at Rio de Janeiro's City Hall. Among those in attendance were the mayor of Rio, the president of the Rio 2016 Summer Games, and leaders of Rio's Jewish community.

"Thank you to Thomas Bach for having helped put an end to years of abject indifference regarding the memory of these innocent victims of '72," said José Serra, Brazil's foreign minister. "It is an honor for me to speak on behalf of President Temer and the Brazilian government in this ceremony, painful as it may be to recall the tragic events that bring us together this evening. Brazil rejects terrorism in any and all of its forms. No justification whatsoever exists for such crimes, and the civilized world shall never accept and never forget actions such as the Munich massacre."

As symbols of remembrance, eleven flames in gilded torches were set alight by Brazilian and Israeli dignitaries, Jewish Brazilian athletes, and Israeli Olympic medalists Yael Arad and Oren Smadja.

"This remembrance is our solemn responsibility that we owe to the victims," said Dr. Bach in his address.

A week later, during the Rio Games' Closing Ceremony, a moment of reflection was offered for those who had died during the Olympics. Israel's Olympic team returned home from Rio with two bronze medals in judo.

"All these years of struggling and fighting—from the moment Bach said there'd be a moment of silence in Rio and the memorial in Munich, now I feel I can rest," said Ilana during filming for the documentary in 2014. "Finally, after all these years. What's happened is a big present for us. Thank God, and thank you Thomas Bach."

CHAPTER 6

A SACRED SITE

> *"The memorial site is a green, hilly park used by all kinds of people. We want to show that terrorist attacks are attacks against ordinary people living out their everyday lives."*
>
> –Werner Karg, director of the Munich 1972 Massacre Memorial project

MORE THAN FORTY YEARS of effort were finally paying off. Thanks to enormous breakthroughs with the German government and the IOC, the families of the eleven had been granted access to the Bavarian Archives and had been honored with a moment of silence at the Olympic Games. They had one last goal to see to fruition—the construction of the Munich 1972 Massacre Memorial in the Olympic Village, something they felt was important not only for them and their loved ones but for generations to come.

"We had a lot of proposals to build it at the Fürstenfeldbruck airport, which is forty-five minutes away from the Olympic Village," said Ankie Spitzer. "We insisted that we would not have any memorial but in the Olympic Village. Lots of people come to the Olympic Village and want to see where it happened. They kept telling us it was impossible, and I said, 'If it won't be there, then don't bother, because that's where it should be. That's where it happened, that's where people come to see it.' Suddenly, we heard it would be realized, and I was thrilled, not only me but all of the families. There's finally going to be a respectable, appropriate memorial in the Olympic Village."

"It was very important for me that the memorial would be built near the Olympic field and the area where my father was killed," said Michal Shahar.

The memorial is situated within a place with multiple sight lines toward 31 Connollystrasse, the Olympic Stadium, the media hill, and Fürstenfeldbruck.

"Not only for me, but for people all over the world to understand that the Olympic Games are international, not political, and if something political happened, we need to be reminded that that's not what the Games are about. It's very important to have a place where everybody can remember."

OLYMPIAPARK TODAY

Since the 1972 Munich Games, Olympiapark's attractions, including its stadium, swimming pools, ice rink, tennis courts, and grassy knolls, have continued to be a focal point of the local community for sporting events, cultural attractions, and other activities. The Olympic Village has since become a residential community, and now the blue doors and window frames of the former Israeli compound peek out from behind leafy curtains of green ivy.

After months of discussion, the Munich

Construction for the Munich 1972 Massacre Memorial began in November of 2015.

The Munich 1972 Massacre Memorial under construction

1972 Massacre Memorial project team finally settled on a location in the heart of Munich's Olympiapark.

"There was a lot of discussion with local residents about exact location," said Ankie, "but we said we'll go along with whatever you propose as long as it's in the Olympic Village, and not somewhere way out where nobody will understand why it is there. Local people didn't want to be reminded. But it happened here. You can't build it miles away. I understand you don't want it in your backyard, but it happened here."

"When the idea of the memorial came up, some of the people who live in the former Olympic Village buildings were against any new construction in this park, but we've been committed to seeing this project come to fruition," explained Michael Bader, the academic assistant for the Munich 1972 Massacre Memorial project, who was born the year of the attacks in his hometown. "It's not a big, ugly thing but graded with the landscape—

beautiful and low profile. After forty-plus years, the City of Munich and the State of Bavaria feel it's important to do this memorial, and to do it right."

During our many trips to Munich for project planning meetings, we visited the grassy, undulating landscape where the memorial now stands. Surrounded by beautiful trees, the site sits to the east of the Olympic Stadium and south of the former Israeli compound.

"The memorial site is a green, hilly park used by all kinds of people," said Werner Karg, director of the Munich 1972 Massacre Memorial project. "The terrorist attack was an attack against the free world, an attack against sports, an attack against international coming-together. It was an attack on the Israelis, but also on the spirit of the Games and everyone who was a part of it. We want to show that terrorist attacks are attacks against ordinary people living out their everyday lives, and these people have a right to live their lives free and unharmed."

THE ARCHITECTURE OF MEMORY

"Our design catches remembrance like a pot or container, and on the other hand, our place of remembrance is wide and open. Openness, and open-mindedness, allow new ways of remembrance."

—Peter Brückner, architect,
Brückner & Brückner Architekten

GIVEN THAT THE FOUNDATION for Global Sports has been extensively involved in the Olympic community, Dr. Bach asked us to join the Munich 1972 Massacre Memorial project team and serve as a liaison between the various parties involved. In 2014, we were honored to sit in on many hours of meetings with the Israeli and German delegations and a room full of brilliant architects. Six architectural firms and exhibition designers from Bavaria, Berlin, Vienna, and Tel Aviv were invited to participate in the competitive bid. The jury tasked with selecting a design was made up of twelve voting members and eight additional consultants. Among the dozen voting members of the jury, there were three architects, one landscape architect, several German government representatives, and Israel's consul general. The jury's interests and perspectives were therefore pluralistic and diverse.

As advisors and consultants, we asked questions and spoke about our impressions of the presentations and mockups of the landscape and memorial design. We were fascinated by the ways these designers explored the architecture of memory, mourning, and reconciliation and proposed ways a structure could pull people together.

Barbara Holzer, a world-renowned Swiss architect with extensive experience in cultural museums and historical exhibits, chaired the jury and moderated the presentations. She played a key role in translating diverse design ideas to the evaluation committee.

"As the chair of the jury, it was crucial for me to listen to all of the different opinions and perspectives," said

David Ulich and Steven Ungerleider attended the opening of the Munich 1972 Massacre Memorial on September 6, 2017. (Matan Radin)

Holzer. "In the end, however, you have to reach a consensus that every member of the jury can support. In this role, I had to take into account diverse expectations, and it was my responsibility to ensure those expectations were met, and if not, explain why."

The selection process went through three phases. In the first round, three out of the original six plans were eliminated,

Barbara Holzer (Thomas Müller)

and in the second round, the number was reduced to two project proposals. During each round, intensive discussions focused on key aspects of the proposed designs in order to reach a final decision. Those issues included how the proposed designs interacted with the landscape with reference to the crime site; how well the designs covered and protected the place where historic and biographical information would be presented; whether the space allowed a forum for groups to meet, discuss, and reflect; and whether the designs possessed the qualities of both a place for education and information, as well as a dignified memorial.

"A memorial has to be a site that gives room to societal and individual reflection. A memorial site ideally should provide a space for thought and information that doesn't patronize or dominate its visitors," explained Holzer. "While discussing the different project propositions intensely, we listed pros and cons and eventually reached a consensus on which projects best met the vision we shared. The jury's dialogue was crucial

for understanding and respecting a wide range of criteria. Each and every one of the submitted projects contributed to the discussion and to forming opinions that led to the final decision. Thus, all submitted entries were important for the memorial-building process."

The winning design came from the Bavarian firm Brückner & Brückner Architects, headed by brothers Peter and Christian Brückner, who partnered with cultural scientist Dr. Winfried Helm on the presentation. This project was a prestigious bid to win, one that carried with it a great sense of honor in a unique field of architecture.

"It was absolutely amazing for us to have been invited to this very special architectural competition," said Peter Brückner, who we interviewed during the making of the *Munich '72 and Beyond* documentary. "We had great respect for this task and this chance to do this very special thing. We had a long discussion and spent many hours working on this very special draft. When we received the

Designed by Brückner & Brückner, the memorial's open spaces allow for both individuals and groups to gather and reflect on the tragedy in Munich. (Matan Radin)

news that we won the competition, it was for our team, my brother and me, a special moment, and we were very happy. It was a great honor to do this work."

The architects invited to bid, explained Brückner, were given technical and factual requirements for the exhibition and the structural concept. Part of their challenge was to ensure that the memorial was clearly visible from all sides, was hard to

vandalize, and focused not only on the victims' biographies, but also offered a deeper understanding of the political and historical context of the terrorist attack.

In describing his creative process, Brückner said that, at the beginning of the project, his team searched for traces and clues within the landscape—as if the topography of the site location would tell them what to do.

"My brother and I walked around Olympic Park for many hours discussing how to find the right answer for this place and this task, and we always asked what wanted to be on this special place," he said.

The result was a design that stood in stark contrast to the five other presentations—the defining feature is its placement as a deep cut into the hillside. The mound of the hill functions as the memorial's rooftop, upheld at the center by a black, V-shaped pillar. Underneath the roof is about 1,700 square feet of exhibition space, open on three sides and freely accessible twenty-four hours a day. Wide, shallow concrete steps lead down into the memorial, inviting visitors to linger. The atmosphere under the roof fosters concentration and contemplation while remaining connected to the openness outside.

"Remembrance was our intention; pausing for a moment was an important factor as well," said Brückner. "Our design catches remembrance like a pot or container, and on the other hand, our place of remembrance is wide and open. Openness, and open-mindedness, allow new ways of remembrance."

What makes the memorial's design especially poignant is how the architecture itself embodies the psychology of mourning and grief. The memorial disrupts the scenery in a way that has a highly symbolic and metaphorical value. In some cultures, when families bury their dead, they rip or cut clothing to symbolize the pain of the loss—the cut to the very heart of their being. Central to the design's thematic concept, the "cut" into the hill carries this same profound meaning—the lives of the athletes and police officer cut down and an empty space left in the lives of everyone who cared about them.

"The assassination in 1972 was a break, a turning point, and the cut is for us a center symbol for a dramatic, long, effective incident," Brückner explained. "Deep feelings, depression, human scale, solid information—those are the

A black, V-shaped pillar features biographies of the eleven Israeli athletes and the German police officer. (Matan Radin)

guiding principles for our draft. This place of remembrance respects what is already there. Nothing is added, but something is taken away and transformed—this is the cut. Just as this happened during the tragic Olympics in 1972, the physical cut through the hill manifests this idea."

Brückner & Brückner's winning submission, noted Holzer, had an abstract,

emblematic quality that succeeded at interweaving symbolism with educational information.

"The roof is about defining space," said Holzer, during interviews for the documentary. "In my eyes, the question is, 'What spaces are really spaces of memory, and how can you get a certain concentration so that a space of memory opens up in a particular space?' It's different from

A view of the Munich Olympic stadium from beneath the memorial's roof. (Matan Radin)

classical land art, where you have the landscape interact with certain elements. In this design, the landscape is more like the container. It's not an addition; it's a sort of negative moment. I think that was very convincing."

The roof, described Holzer, creates a concentrated, protective space even in the middle of the outdoors, offering a moment of retreat and contemplation while limiting a visitor's distractions.

"The cut is very symbolic and the idea is very abstract," she added. "In this organic landscape built for the Olympic Games, the cut is something very brutal, precise, dramatic; it's a juxtaposition with that organic landscape. It's a very silent but precise thought."

Though it holds deep symbolic meaning, Brückner & Brückner's design is meant to impact everyday people on a visceral level. By evoking emotion and curiosity,

The rooftop's design gives the impression the memorial was cut out of the hill—both part of the landscape and yet set apart from it. (Matan Radin)

the architecture compels visitors to enter and explore the space within. Visitors then take in the narratives and content presented in the exhibit, which shoulders the legacy of the victims by placing significant focus on their individual life stories.

Against the back of the exhibition area is the Media Wall, an LED display about thirty-six feet long, which chronicles the events of the massacre through an ongoing twenty-five-minute loop of news footage. The Media Wall employs the most advanced technology available and is protected by safety glass. The black triangular column in the center of the space displays the biographies of the eleven fallen athletes and the slain German police officer. Included in the exhibit are personal effects that belonged to each victim of the attack.

"The most important aim of this memorial is to remember the twelve victims," noted Spaenle. "We will give the victims back their names, their personality, their identity near the place where they died."

"We personalize the victims and show them as human beings—as people like you and me," said Brückner.

"Identifying the names of the Israeli athletes says, 'You are someone. You are a person that represented your country and trained. You are an Olympian.' I think it's a hugely significant acknowledgment of an athlete's place in the world," said Barry Maister. "Being an Olympian is a defining moment in your life. That's why I think this memorial is so fitting because it's going to be there forever to declare that those people matter, and their memory will now have less chance of being forgotten."

While the victims and the families they left behind are the prime focus of the memorial, the historical and political context is crucial for gaining a deeper understanding of the terrorist attack in Munich.

"Though I remember this day, many on our team have no direct memory of the attack," said Brückner. "We asked them,

Visitors read biographies and view news footage along the LED media display. (Matan Radin)

'What would interest you on this?' And those ideas went into our draft. It is a question which we need to ask and spread throughout the whole world."

The memorial's Media Wall presents not only the story of the terrorist attack, but also the political dimensions of the 1972 Munich Games, the significance of the 1972 Summer Games for Germany, the Arab-Israeli conflict, the reasons Black September used the Olympics to make

a brutal political statement, and the emergence of international terrorism.

The project team created the memorial within a place with historical sight lines—one of imagination to Fürstenfeldbruck, one viewable line to 31 Connollystrasse, one to the Olympic Stadium, one to the grassy hill where the media gathered, one toward the Fritz Koenig sculpture, and so on, in every direction. When visitors stand before the Media Wall, they can interact with the educational materials, while looking out beyond the space toward one of the sight lines to place the events in real-life context.

"The memorial is clearly against terrorism and brutality," said Holzer. "Diplomatic ideas are important—it's about the values of a democratic society, the respect of people, of different cultures, of different religions. It's the best you can give people: to open their minds for just a moment in their busy lives, to let them pause and think about the importance of peace."

"The memorial is clearly against terrorism and brutality. Diplomatic ideas are important–it's about the values of a democratic society, the respect of people, of different cultures, of different religions. It's the best you can give people: to open their minds for just a moment in their busy lives, to let them pause and think about the importance of peace." –Barbara Holzer, architect and lead jurist on the Munich Massacre Memorial project

---

LOOKING TOWARD THE FUTURE

The Munich Massacre Memorial project is one of the most important and meaningful undertakings that we have had the privilege to be a part of. After our four decades of involvement with the Olympic movement, we sensed just how overdue it was that we appropriately memorialize the victims and hopefully bring a sense of closure to their families.

"Forty years is about the right time, because it's about a generation, and new questions come from new generations— from those who may not have all lived through it," noted Brückner. "It's now the right time to do it in this place with the people who remember, including the victims' families, so you can discuss with them, and put it in this place, and transform it for the next generation."

"The Holocaust, Munich, 9/11—these things need to be remembered," said Noam Schiller, former Israeli special operative and security expert. "People should be reminded about the situation and the fragility of life, and should do

לזכר קורבנות הפיגוע באולימפיאדת מינכן

Erinnerungsort
Olympia-Attentat München 1972
Munich 1972 Massacre Memorial

The Foundation for Global Sports Development provided a financial grant toward the memorial's construction and participated in the process of choosing a winning design. (Matan Radin)

whatever we can that things like this won't happen again. A memorial like this in Munich now—I think it's better late than sorry. It's better that it's there."

A groundbreaking ceremony on the memorial site was held in November of 2015, and construction continued for almost two years. This inspiring memorial sets a precedent for how to best honor and remember those who have made the ultimate sacrifice. Ultimately, the Munich 1972 Massacre Memorial is a very human story, an empowering story, one that not only honors those who have gone before us, but also offers wisdom for future generations.

"We want everyone to come," said Brückner during our interviews in 2014. "This place of remembrance should be a place for the victims and their families, for our contemporaries, as well as the younger generations—student groups and educational exchanges, for example. Everybody should also get information about the Olympic Games, the assassination, and the impact of terrorism from this place.

Everybody should take a small piece of remembrance from here."

"A public memorial like this one is where remembrance physically manifests. I hope visitors to the memorial will understand there's always a before and an after, and you never know exactly where you are," said Holzer. "Before this crime happened, the landscape was a joyful, innocent place, and in that moment, everything changed. I want people to understand what a moment can do—to life, to politics, to friendship."

Though the memorial can't bring back their loved ones, the survivors of the Israeli athletes deeply appreciate its purpose as a permanent place of remembrance.

"I'm very happy about the new memorial. It will give a chance to so many people to come and know what happened, and to remember every sportsman that got killed," said Mika Slavin. "My daughter is very excited. She says, 'We have to go and see that!' I will go with my kids

Israeli president Reuven Rivlin (third from left) shakes hands with German president Frank-Walter Steinmeier (center) as they pose with wife of German president Elke Buedenbender (L-R), the Israeli president's wife Nehama Rivlin, Bavarian State Premier Horst Seehofer and his wife Karin Seehofer, and Bavaria's minister of culture Ludwig Spaenle during the inauguration of the Munich Massacre Memorial. (Joerg Koch/Getty Images)

to visit and to see my brother there with all his friends, and it's just beautiful to know that it was built for them."

"This is the story of my life," said Oshrat Romano Kandell. "For me this memorial is my father. All the symbols, this is my father now. The memorial helps me to remember the father who was an athlete, who represented Israel at the Olympic Games, and for my children to be proud. The memorial is going to be life, like a heartbeat. It will be something that will give life to those who visit, in a way that my children and their children will remember."

"Now I understand that this attack, it's important for people," said Shahar. "It wasn't just, 'They killed my father and ten others, and oh, it's okay.' It matters to other people also—it's important that everybody understands this. I feel very fulfilled."

"It should have happened a long time ago, but I'm very happy it's there now so that future generations will also understand what happened and how to work together so it doesn't happen again," said Ankie. "If the memorial in the Olympic Village in Munich can fulfill our aim of instilling the Olympic spirit—brotherhood, peace, friendship—it will be one of the happiest things in my life."

After more than four decades of fighting for justice and recognition, the families of the eleven expressed how relieved they were to see this long chapter of their lives finally come to a close.

"These men were the sons of the Olympics, and this memorial will be something to remember them for years," said Ilana Romano. "There are still things I

have to do, but after more than forty years of struggle, I would like to rest."

"Beyond the memorial, the goal is to keep living and to keep enjoying our lives and not to get stuck in the tragedy and drama," said Alex Springer. "Most of all, we want to live a normal life."

IN MEMORIAM

The Munich Massacre Memorial officially opened with a special ceremony on September 6, 2017, on the forty-fifth anniversary of the shoot-out at Fürstenfeldbruck airfield. Those of us with the Foundation for Global Sports Development, including Dr. Steven Ungerleider, David Ulich, Kelly Crabb, Paul Malingagio, Michael Cascio, and other executives, were honored to attend the opening ceremony. Among the attendees were German and Israeli dignitaries, the families of the fallen athletes, and other guests who had gathered to commemorate two historic occasions—the anniversary of the massacre and the opening of the long-awaited memorial.

World leaders including Reuven Rivlin,

David Ulich and Dr. Thomas Bach (Matan Radin)

president of Israel, Frank-Walter Stein-meier, president of the Federal Republic of Germany, and IOC president Dr. Thomas Bach gave touching speeches that included mild apologies for the long wait, the denial, and the politics that had surrounded the perpetual delay in the memorial's construction. Ronald S. Lauder, president of the World Jewish Congress, spoke about rampant anti-Semitism and the ongoing struggle with terrorism in many parts of the world.

In his address, Dr. Ungerleider acknowl-edged the victims, the IOC, Dr. Bach, and the Bavarian officials, including Werner Karg, Michael Bader, and Dr. Ludwig Spaenle. He also acknowl-edged his colleagues at the Founda-tion for Global Sports Development, including his longtime associate of thirty years, David Ulich, for his vision and perseverance on the Munich Me-morial Project.

"This whole experience has been bitter-sweet and somewhat surreal," said Dr. Ungerleider, who was accompanied by his partner, Joanna Rice, and his two daughters, Dr. Shoshana Ungerleider and Dr. Ariel Ungerleider Kelley. "Here we are after forty-five years of wandering in the desert, waiting for the IOC and other powerful players to acknowledge the horrific murders in 1972. And now, the memorial as a place to worship and give honor has come to fruition—a small but crucial step toward closure of this enormous wound. It is all still hard to grasp and internalize."

In her closing remarks, Ankie Spitzer said, "Forty-five years is a long time coming. I'm grateful for this moment, but we still have work to do." She finished by noting that the German government had lied to the victims' families, and she asked for additional inquiry into the archives that remain under lock and key.

NOTE FROM THE AUTHORS

As we embarked on this journey nearly five years ago, we could never have imagined the impact it would have on our lives and our futures. When IOC president Dr. Thomas Bach asked us to serve as liaison between the various parties involved in the Munich Massacre Memorial, we were honored to accept such a profoundly important role. We will be forever grateful for the opportunity Dr. Bach presented, the experiences that were born, and the relationships that were forged. More than anything, we are thankful that we had the ability to give the victims' families a voice and a safe place to share their stories.

Participating in the architectural competitions was moving enough to influence the creation of our documentary film, *Munich '72 and Beyond*. We were involved in the entirety of the production process—from research and development to post-production. As first-time filmmakers, the experience itself was unbelievable. We loved every minute of it—the good, the bad, the ugly, even the moments when we thought we were completely in over our heads. Because, at the end of it all, there is nothing more profound than the awe-inspiring and powerful feeling you get when you witness the transformative power of healing—it's breathtaking.

May we all do something in our own way to leave behind a legacy of making the world just a little bit better.

Dr. Steven Ungerleider and David Ulich
SEPTEMBER 6, 2017

HORST SEEHOFER

Five years ago, I announced the plan to create a place of remembrance in honor of the victims of the Munich massacre. Now that project has become reality. The incision in the grounds of Olympia Park creates a space of information and meditation. And it reminds us of a crime that inflicted an injury on our day and age.

The attack on the Israeli team shocked the world. Eleven athletes and one policeman fell victim to terrorists. The pain of that loss still burdens the families today. The surviving members of the team still suffer from the experience of the event.

For those reasons, it was a matter of heartfelt concern to me to light a beacon of sympathy. We wanted there to be a clear symbol of the bond we feel with all who lost relatives and friends in 1972.

I hope the Place of Remembrance will fulfill this purpose. I would like to thank the City of Munich, the Federal Republic of Germany, the International Olympic Committee, the Foundation for Global Sports Development, and the German Olympic Sports Confederation for supporting our project. I am especially indebted to the guests of honor and the representatives of the State of Israel standing side by side with us today!

— Horst Seehofer
MINISTER-PRESIDENT OF BAVARIA,
SEPTEMBER 6, 2017

SANDRA SIMOVICH

The opportunity to participate in the opening of the Munich 1972 Massacre Memorial just three weeks after taking office as the new consul general represents the apex of my career to date, both professionally and personally. And the presence of the Israeli president Reuven Rivlin and his wife, Nechama Rivlin, testifies to the outstanding importance of this event for Israel.

The participation of the Israeli athletes in the 1972 Summer Olympics was intended as a strong symbol of the increasing normalization of relations between our two countries. Then, however, the Games were overshadowed by terror and murder—a traumatic experience for Israel and Germany alike, and a cruel blow to the peaceful idea of the Olympic Games.

What makes the Place of Remembrance so special is that it focuses on the human beings and their personal stories. The murder victims are not mere names, but husbands, fathers, and sons. The new exhibition conveys this aspect in a very convincing manner.

Every successful project needs people who firmly believe in it—and we had and have such people. I would like to thank all partners and supporters most sincerely for recognizing the importance of this project and for furthering its progress with the utmost dedication, even in difficult situations.

— Sandra Simovich,
CONSUL GENERAL OF THE
STATE OF ISRAEL FOR SOUTHERN GERMANY,
SEPTEMBER 6, 2017

ABOUT THE AUTHORS

STEVEN UNGERLEIDER, PhD, is an internationally recognized research psychologist, Olympic consultant, and author of six books. His most notable work is *Faust's Gold: Inside the East German Doping Machine*, a look at how the corrupt, state-sponsored sports organizations of East Germany dominated international athletics by giving unsuspecting athletes massive doses of performance-enhancing drugs. *Faust's Gold* won several awards, was used in Senate drug hearings, and became a PBS special entitled *Doping for Gold: Secrets of the Dead*. Along with David Ulich, Dr. Ungerleider was nominated for an Emmy in the category of Outstanding Research for the *Munich '72 and Beyond* film at the 38th Annual News and Documentary Emmy Awards.

Dr. Ungerleider is also vice president of the Foundation for Global Sports Development. He has served on the education and ethics panel of the World Anti-Doping Agency, the education committee of the International Paralympic Committee, and on the advisory panel of the American Psychological Association. Dr. Ungerleider was also chief mediator in the doping case between Lance Armstrong and Olympic Cycling. For more about Dr. Ungerleider's work, visit stevenungerleider.com.

DAVID ULICH, JD, LLM, is on the executive board of the Foundation for Global Sports development, through which he has worked closely with the International Olympic Committee, the International Paralympic Committee, and the US Olympic Committee on sports development programs throughout the world. Along with Dr. Steven Ungerleider, Ulich was nominated for an Emmy in the category of Outstanding Research for the *Munich '72 and Beyond* film at the 38th Annual News and Documentary Emmy Awards.

Ulich is an advocate for the integrity of sports, the Olympic Games, and athletes endangered by performance-enhancing drugs. He serves on the boards of the US Olympic Committee Foundation, the Southern California Committee for the Olympic Games, the LA 2028 Olympic Games Bid Committee, and the International Committee for Fair Play. Ulich is a partner of the law firm Sheppard, Mullin,

Richter & Hampton LLP and leads the firm's nonprofit sector team. For more on Ulich's expertise, visit sheppardmullin.com/dulich.

ABOUT THE FILMMAKERS

MICHAEL CASCIO was the programming chief at National Geographic Channel, served as VP at NBC News during which time he created a documentary strategy for MSNBC, and helped launch the History Channel while at A&E. His work has covered hard-hitting topics from the Holocaust to 9/11. In his noteworthy career in documentary television programming, Cascio has garnered four Emmys, two Oscar nominations, and a Producer of the Year award. Cascio now advises selected media and production partners through his company, M&C Media LLC. To learn more about Cascio's work, visit mandcmedia.com/team.

STEPHEN CRISMAN is a writer, director, and producer whose credits include prestigious programs for A&E, History, MSNBC, and CBS's *60 Minutes*. Crisman Films has earned an Emmy Award, seven Emmy nominations, multiple Cable Ace and Banff nominations, as well as screenings at the Berlin Film Festival and several others.

ABOUT THE FOUNDATION FOR GLOBAL SPORTS DEVELOPMENT

Founded in 1994, the Foundation for Global Sports Development (GSD) strives to be a leader in the international sports community by delivering and supporting initiatives that promote fair play, education, and the physical, emotional, and developmental benefits of sports for youth around the world. GSD places special emphasis on constituencies most in need or least served by current programs, including women, minorities, and at-risk youth. GSD works closely with the US Olympic Committee, the IOC, various sports federations, and committed athletes on programs and initiatives that promote sportsmanship and ethics, including a mentorship outreach that takes youngsters to the Olympic Games. For more on GSD's mission and programs, visit globalsportsdevelopment.org.

The Foundation for
Global Sports Development

1. Tim Naftali, "The Lessons of Munich 1972," *Blind Spot: The Secret History of American Counterterrorism* (New York: Basic Books, 2009), 55.

2. "Terrorism: Horror and Death at the Olympics," Time, Monday, September 18, 1972, http://content.time.com /time/subscriber/article/0,33009,906384-1,00.html

3. Tim Naftali, "The Lessons of Munich 1972," *Blind Spot: The Secret History of American Counterterrorism* (New York: Basic Books, 2009), 57-58.

4. United States Holocaust Memorial Museum, Holocaust Encyclopedia, ttps://www.ushmm.org/wlc/en/article. php?ModuleId=10007087, accessed August 25, 2017.

5. United States Holocaust Memorial Museum, Holocaust Encyclopedia, https://www.ushmm.org/wlc/en/article. php?ModuleId=10005680, accessed August 25, 2017.

6. *Ibid.*

7. Simon Reeve, *One Day in September: The Full Story of the 1972 Munich Olympics Massacre* (New York: Arcade Publishing, 2000), xi.

8. Alexander Wolff, "When the Terror Began Thirty Years Later, the Hostage Drama That Left 11 Israeli Olympians Dead Seems Even More Chilling and Offers Grim Reminders to Today's Security Experts," *Sports Illustrated*, August 26, 2002.

9. *Ibid.*

10. From his interview for *1972*, a film by Sarah Morris, 2008.

11. Simon Reeve, *One Day in September: The Full Story of the 1972 Munich Olympics Massacre* (New York: Arcade Publishing, 2000), 123.

12. Encyclopedia Brittanica, "Munich Massacre," https://www.britannica.com/event/Munich-Massacre, accessed August 25, 2017.

13. Aaron J. Klein, *Striking Back: The 1972 Munich Olympics Massacre and Israel's Deadly Response* (New York: Random House, 2007), 126.

14. *Id.*, 128. Jason Burke, "Bonn 'faked' hijack to free killers," *The Guardian*, March 25, 2000, https:// www.theguardian.com/world/2000/mar/26/ jasonburke.theobserver1.
     DasErste.de, "Wie die Olympia-Attentäter unbestraft davonkamen," June 18, 2013, http://archive.is/wweOv.

15. ABC Sports/ESPN, *The Tragedy of the Munich Games*, 2005.

16. *Ibid.*

17. National Park Service, "David Berger Sculpture," https://www.nps.gov/dabe/learn/historyculture/david-berger-sculpture.htm, accessed August 25, 2017.

18. Hillel Kuttler, "From Darkness of Munich Olympics, Moments of Clarity," *New York Times*, August 4, 2012.

19. Biography courtesy of the Munich 1972 Massacre Memorial project team.

20. "Ze'ev Friedman," The Munich Eleven, http://www.themunicheleven.com/indexzf.html, accessed August 25, 2017.

21. Information courtesy of the Munich 1972 Massacre Memorial project team.

22. Alan Abrahamson, "Black September," *Los Angeles Times*, September 5, 2002.

23. *Ibid.*

24. Information courtesy of the Munich 1972 Massacre Memorial project team.

25. *Ibid.*

26. From a private video, https://www.youtube.com/watch?v=qateuIRaQ7E, accessed August 25, 2017.

27. Information courtesy of the Munich 1972 Massacre Memorial project team.

28. *Ibid.*

29. Alan Abrahamson, "Black September," *Los Angeles Times*, September 5, 2002.

30. Information courtesy of the Munich 1972 Massacre Memorial project team.

31. *Ibid.*

32. *Ibid.*

33. *Ibid.*